REAGANOMICS AND AFTER

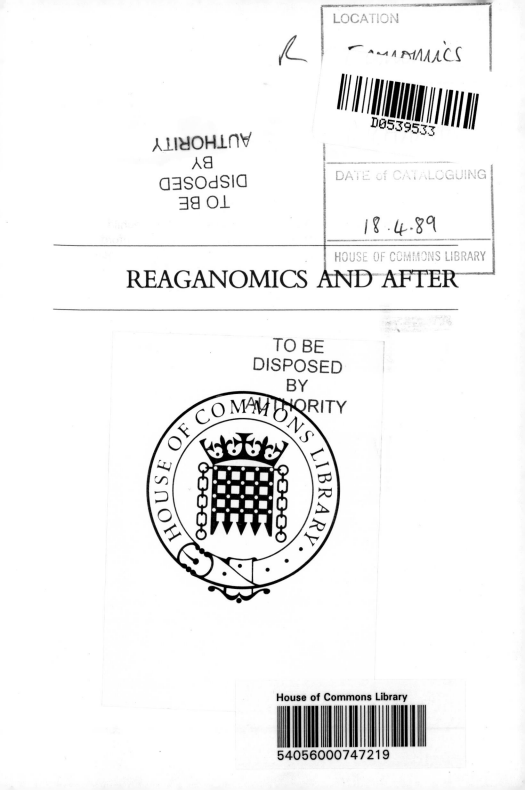

REAGANOMICS
AND AFTER

James M Buchanan · William A Niskanen

Paul Craig Roberts · Patrick Minford

Irwin Stelzer · Alan Budd

Introduced by
Sir Alan Peacock

IEA
Institute of Economic Affairs
1989

First published in February 1989
by
THE INSTITUTE OF ECONOMIC AFFAIRS
2 Lord North Street, Westminster, London SW1P 3LB

IEA Readings 28

ISSN 0305-814X
ISBN 0-255 36219-6

Printed in Great Britain by
Goron Pro-Print Co. Ltd., Lancing, W. Sussex
Filmset in 'Berthold' Times Roman 11 on 12 point

CONTENTS

FOREWORD

Cento Veljanovski
Research & Editorial Director,
Institute of Economic Affairs

THE ECONOMIC PERFORMANCE of the US economy has major and wide-ranging effects on the world economy. President Reagan entered office with a bold policy of supply-side reforms which was subsequently labelled 'Reaganomics'. In *Readings 28* a distinguished group of economists from both sides of the Atlantic assesses Reaganomics and compares it with the economic policy of Mrs Thatcher's Government.

Reaganomics and After collects together the papers delivered at a conference co-sponsored by the Cato Institute (Washington DC) and the IEA held in London on 8 December 1988. The conference began with a Special Lecture by Professor James M. Buchanan, Nobel Laureate in Economics, which sets the Reagan years in a public-choice framework. Professor Sir Alan Peacock has, at the IEA's invitation, written an Introduction which ties together the themes developed by the contributors.

It therefore only remains for me to issue the disclaimer that as an educational trust the IEA dissociates itself from the views and opinions of its authors who write in their own capacity as independent scholars and experts.

February 1989

CENTO VELJANOVSKI
Research & Editorial Director

ix

INTRODUCTION:
Some Methodological Questions

Alan Peacock
Executive Director,
The David Hume Institute

INTRODUCTION

THE CONTRIBUTIONS in this *Readings* are provided by a posse of very well known experts in the appraisal of economic policies. They have in common that they all have international professional reputations, that they are broadly sympathetic to both Reaganite and Thatcherite policies, and they have helped to formulate or to influence those policies, some from outside and some from inside the government machine. They are uniquely placed to pronounce upon Reaganomics and After.

I have acceded to the wishes of the IEA that I write an Introduction only because it enables me to express my appreciation to the authors in a particular form, that is by drawing the reader's attention to the important questions they raise about the methodology of appraising economic policies.

A stylised version of the procedure[1] appraising the economic performance of a government would go something like this:

---

[1] A very good example of this approach which is particularly apposite to our discussion is to be found in Nobel Prizewinner Franco Modigliani's 'Reagan's Economic Policy: A Critique', *Oxford Economic Papers*, Vol. 40, No 3, September 1988.

(a) Identify the main economic objectives of government, their relative importance and their expression in quantitative form;

(b) identify some 'model' of the economy which explains how it works as expressed in quantitative relationships in which the indices denoting the objectives (e.g., the rates of growth, inflation and unemployment) are clearly identified;

(c) identify the policy instruments (e.g., fiscal and monetary variables) which the government is assumed to control;

(d) determine the 'degree of success' of the government in the use of the instruments in order to reach the previously identified objectives having regard to the constraints imposed on government action by the reactions of the various parts of the private sector to government attempts to influence economic behaviour.

Giving content to the various 'stages of production' of an appraisal reveals some interesting differences in approach by the authors represented in this volume, however similar their philosophical outlook and analytical apparatus, and which will now be explored.

THE CHOICE OF OBJECTIVES

It has become widely accepted, and, in general, our authors agree, that the choice of objectives is solved by identifying target variables, movements in which denote an increase or decrease in society's welfare. Thus, traditionally, there are three targets identified as of particular importance: the rate of economic growth, the unemployment rate and the rate of inflation, the welfare of society being a positive function of the first variable and a negative function of the second and third variables. With the government as the 'agenda setter', policy success consists in taking credit for favourable movements in the target variables. However, the problem of appraisal is complicated by the difficulties encountered in identifying what are *feasible* movements in these variables over the planning period of the government and by the mode of choice of the 'trade-offs' between one variable and another: how is an 'adverse' movement in prices to be compared with a 'favourable' movement in employment?

A remarkable feature of these papers is the concentration on the means rather than the ends of policy. The authors have an understandable distaste for identifying targets in a way which would commit

IEA PUBLICATIONS
Subscription Service

An annual subscription is the most convenient way to obtain our publications. Every title we produce in all our regular series will be sent to you immediately on publication and without further charge, representing a substantial saving.

Individual subscription rates*

Britain: £25·00 p.a. including postage.
£23·00 p.a. if paid by Banker's Order.
£15·00 p.a. to teachers and students who pay *personally.*

Europe: £25·00 p.a. including postage.

South America: £35·00 p.a. or equivalent.

Other Countries: Rates on application. In most countries subscriptions are handled by local agents. Addresses are available from the IEA.

* These rates are *not* available to companies or to institutions.

To: The Treasurer, Institute of Economic Affairs,
2 Lord North Street, Westminster,
London SW1P 3LB

I should like to subscribe from ....

I enclose a cheque/postal order for:

☐ £25·00

☐ £15·00   I am a teacher/student at ....

....

☐ Please send a Banker's Order form.

☐ Please send an invoice.

☐ Please charge my credit card:

Please tick ☐ 𝗩𝗜𝗦𝗔 ☐ ◣ ☐ AMERICAN EXPRESS ☐ ◍

Card No: ┌─┬─┬─┬─┬─┬─┬─┬─┬─┬─┬─┬─┬─┬─┬─┬─┐
         └─┴─┴─┴─┴─┴─┴─┴─┴─┴─┴─┴─┴─┴─┴─┴─┘

In addition I would like to purchase the following previously published titles:

....

....

Name ....⎫

Address ....⎬ BLOCK LETTERS PLEASE

....

.... Post Code ....⎭

Signed .... Date ....

RPE28

the US or UK governments to an agenda reminiscent of economic planning models associated with previous régimes. This extends to a sympathy with politicians for not being too specific about their precise objectives, not only, one supposes, because the link between the welfare of individuals and quantitative targets may be a tenuous one, but also because the ability of governments to achieve specific targets is limited. As Alan Budd shows, written statements about precise objectives are embarrassing to governments if circumstances change and the strong emphasis on beating inflation may be more in accord with what governments are capable of achieving than claims to control rather than influence the rate of growth and the rate of unemployment.

A further feature of the choice of targets is the emphasis placed in both Reaganomics and Thatcherism on the reduction in government intervention as an end in itself and not simply as a means to an end. Hopefully, such a reduction would both restore a greater degree of economic freedom, and act as a stimulus to improvement in growth prospects—a very decided difference in the ends-means relationship than that of previous governments.

'Whose Welfare Function . . .?'

This change in emphasis in delineating targets by which to identify the economic aims of government is marked, but still presupposes that the 'agenda setter' is the government in power. This is an entirely defensible approach which has the advantage of being in keeping with the common parlance of public discussion of economic policy in which governments themselves participate. However, public choice economists such as Professor Buchanan and, I suppose, myself are bound to raise some questions about both the positive and normative implications of concentrating on the welfare function of governments. In asking the question, 'Whose welfare function is of most interest?', a public choice analyst might prefer to identify those economic variables of concern to voters in seeking to influence governments in their exercise of power. The policy paradigm is no longer represented by a 'government identifying desirable movements in target variables with designated trade-offs between the variables', but as a bargaining situation between those who supply policies, i.e. politicians, and those who demand them, i.e. voters. Hence Buchanan's emphasis on the role of interest groups as the key element in the future course of US economic policy.

From a normative standpoint, a public choice analyst might argue that the evaluation of policy must review how far there is correspondence between voters' preferences and government actions, as reflected in the size and pattern of government budgets and government regulation. In broad terms, the basic aim of policy is to minimise coercion, with the preferences of each citizen having equal weight. This emphasis on political egalitarianism would call in question the identification of some collective welfare function maximised by government. Thus minimising coercion implies that individuals should not be forced to achieve some collective saving objective, as would be implied in the pursuit of some target rate of economic growth. The rate of economic growth ceases to become an end in itself and is merely the outcome of individual work and saving patterns.

POLICY MODELS AND POLICY INSTRUMENTS

As I have indicated, the interest of our contributors lies less in precise formulation of some evaluation scale by which to judge policy and more in the deployment of a markedly different set of policy instruments from those used by preceding post-war governments. This is particularly noticeable in micro-economic policy. To take an example from my own experience, as Chief Economic Adviser to the Department of Trade and Industry from 1973-76 I lived through the death throes of a Tory government wedded to selective aid policies which prevented adaptation to change and which fostered restrictive practices, a policy embraced with much enthusiasm by their Labour successors from 1974 onwards. I recall sneaking in a clause in a Labour government policy document which expressed one of the main aims of industrial policy as that of making markets for goods and factor services more competitive. At the umpteenth draft, Mr Kaufman, then Minister of State for Industry, spotted this offending clause just before the document was due to be published, remarking that its tenor was contrary to all that the Labour Party stood for!

Our authors are clearly impressed with the commitment of both the Reagan and Thatcher governments to supply-side economics which has stood previous policies on their head. The kernel of the new policy now lay in letting markets exercise their true function as signalling devices which allocate capital and labour and the products and services they produce to their most efficient uses. This called for a reduction of government involvement in the economy both in budgetary and regulatory terms. The authors to a man clearly admire the intentions if not the associated actions of the politicians who embraced supply-side economics, and by implication agree in essentials about the economic model which supports such policies.

The Appeal of Supply-Side Economics

Indeed, the appeal of supply-side economics transcends any difference in view taken about who sets the agenda. Supply-side economics was clearly designed to improve the growth prospects of the economy as viewed from the government standpoint. At the same time, a public choice approach might perceive supply-side economics as an important way of reducing voter-coercion—through reduction in the proportion of taxes and government expenditure to GDP, for example.

It is widely agreed that one of the most spectacular measures designed to 'give the economy back to the people' has been the US Tax Reform Act of 1986 (TRA-86);[2] and it so happens that the economic debate about its supposed effects displays again a difference of approach which depends on who sets the agenda.

The economic thinking behind TRA-86 is admirably summarised in Paul Craig Roberts's contribution below (Chapter 3), so I need say little about it here. Clearly the desirability of the reform rested on giving preference to the efficiency gains claimed for tax reduction over equity effects. Economists of very different standpoints on policy matters agree that the lowering of marginal and average rates of taxation will have a positive effect on the incentives to work, though some have questioned whether any resultant increase in the government deficit would lead to compensating increases in personal saving.[3] The quantitative effects of tax reductions are, however, hotly disputed. It is interesting to note, for example, that Craig Roberts repudiates the

---

[2] A most interesting debate has taken place in the USA about who deserves credit for the thinking behind TRA-86—see the Symposium in the *Journal of Economic Perspectives*, Vol. 1, Summer 1987, particularly the articles by Henry Aaron, Joseph Pechman, James Buchanan and Richard Musgrave, and more recently in Norman B. Ture, 'The Tax Reform Act of 1986: Revolution or Counter-Revolution?', in David Boaz (ed.), *Assessing the Reagan Years*, Washington DC: The Cato Institute, 1988.

[3] Modigliani, *op. cit.*, is one of several critics of the Barro thesis that if the government substitutes debt finance for tax finance, taxpayers will increase their saving in order to offset the implied future tax burdens. His empirical evidence offers support to his criticisms: but see Paul Craig Roberts, *infra.*, for an alternative explanation of the phenomenon of reduced personal savings. For further analysis of the Barro thesis, see Minford, *infra.*, Chapter 4.

suggestion that the supply-side effects of tax reductions were ever perceived by the US administration as having such a marked effect on the incentive to work and therefore on the growth in real incomes that the tax cuts would pay for themselves—the 'Laffer effect'.[4]

'Pavlovian Dog' Syndrome

There is an element of what I have called elsewhere the 'Pavlovian dog' syndrome in the rather mechanistic arguments which underlie the economic effects of taxation. Taxpayers are embodied in models in which they are subject to stimuli in the form of alternative hypothetical tax régimes. Like Pavlov's dog, they can only react passively, having no concourse with their controllers.

The public choice approach to tax analysis has an altogether different emphasis. It takes into account the distribution of gains and losses of a tax régime, such as those embodied in TRA-86, in which rate reductions are combined with a broadening of the tax base.[5] In a majoritarian political setting, the political feedback from taxpayers' perceptions of the changes are likely to promote demands for further fiscal changes, including changes in other taxes or in government expenditure. In the UK, which along with other countries, has followed the US lead in the move to simplify the rate-bracket structure and to reduce income tax rates, such changes, combined with changes in taxes on expenditure, are perceived to have adverse distributional effects. These may make it more difficult for the government to resist the claims of the aged poor and lower-paid public employees for some compensatory treatment.

In sum, whatever view one takes about the record of Reaganomics, a major change has taken place in the professional status of supply-side economic modelling. What was once damned by a fair proportion of respected professional figures in both the UK and USA as a prime example of 'DIY economics', is now regarded at the very least with grudging respect.

---

[4] For a critical analysis of the Laffer-inspired literature see Alan Peacock, 'The Rise and Fall of the Laffer Curve', in D. Bös and B. Friedrich (eds.), *Progressive Taxation*, Proceedings of a Liberty Fund Conference, Vienna, January 1988, Berlin: Springer Verlag, 1989 (forthcoming).

[5] For a succinct and skilful defence of the explanatory value of such an approach, James Buchanan, 'Tax Reform as Political Choice', *Journal of Economic Perspectives*, Vol. 1, Summer 1987, pp.29-35.

RESULTS

The evaluation of the Reagan administration's record presents some interesting methodological puzzles which have already been indicated. I shall not attempt to solve them, if only because solutions obviously depend on the personal value-judgements of the observer. What may help the reader is to categorise the different evaluation methods, which are not mutually exclusive, and some of the problems to which they give rise. I assume, except where otherwise stated, that observers place most weight on inflation, growth and employment performance.

1. *'Compare with previous régimes'.* The most clear commitment to this standard is Niskanen, who argues that the Reagan administration record is much better than that of the Carter administration on inflation, employment and productivity. The Reagan record on the reduction in inflation is not in dispute and 'even the ranks of Tuscany could scarce forbear to cheer'.[6] Niskanen is careful to point out that the growth in productivity was low though better than that experienced in the Carter era.[7] The problem with this approach is that it leaves an unanswerable question: What would have happened if the previous administration had continued in office? Niskanen bravely nails his colours to the mast:

> '[it] is implausible to believe that President Carter or whoever else might have been elected in 1984 could have accomplished as much'.

2. *'Does Performance match Promise?'* It has already been argued, and illustrated in the papers below, that this method of evaluation runs into the difficulty of how to interpret some of the Delphic utterances of administrations about their intentions. Paul Craig Roberts (*infra.*) illustrates very clearly how a mythology of promises can arise. On the other hand, it has been claimed that the Reagan administration had a

---

[6] Modigliani, who, as we have seen, has been sternly critical of aspects of Reaganomics, admits that the attack on inflation was 'unquestionably a significant success' (*op. cit.*, p. 424), though he adds the rider that success was not obtained by the expected means. (Modigliani is a Roman, not Tuscan!)

[7] Some critics have argued that there has been no significant difference in productivity, as measured by real income per head, between the Reagan and Carter eras. See Robert Litan, Robert Lawrence and Charles Schultze, 'Improving American Living Standards', *Brookings Review*, Vol. 7, No. 1, Winter 1988-89.

very clear agenda,[8] particularly that part of it associated with the objective of reducing the size of government and the impact of its regulatory system. There could be much argument about the degree of success of Reagan in fulfilling stated intentions. In the narrow context of getting the government out of people's hair, the record is clearly patchy, with the tax reform as a large plus, but with the failure to control the growth in government spending and the unanticipated large deficits as definite minuses. Nor was conviction matched by performance in the field of deregulation.[9] However, because of the difficulties in ascertaining the precise intentions of government in the whole range of policies with an economic influence, and of translating these intentions into actual policies, this criterion of appraisal is particularly difficult to apply so soon after the period under study.

3. *'How did the record stand up against that of other advanced economies?'* There are only incidental references to comparative international performance in these papers. On the surface, the movement of the indicators denoting inflation, employment and productivity trends would point towards comparative success, but this would be a simplistic view of the value of this measure. One obvious difficulty is that advanced economies are becoming more and more interdependent. Alan Budd illustrates the difficulty that this presents in making international comparisons of performance by his argument that the appreciating dollar in the mid-1980s made it more difficult for the rest of the world to bring its own rate of inflation down. The consequential tightening of fiscal policy in European countries produced the release in the additional resources absorbed by the USA as it ran its large balance-of-payments deficit. But Craig Roberts clearly rejects any suggestion that the degree of success of Reaganomics was in any way dependent on 'sacrifices' made by other countries!

4. *'How far did the record accord with voters' preferences?'* This question cannot be answered without considering the link between voters' perceptions of their welfare and their perceptions of the relative

---

[8] 'No President in this century has come to Washington with a clearer policy agenda than Ronald Reagan, or so the story goes', remarks David Boaz. See his 'Introduction' to *Assessing the Reagan Years, op. cit.*

[9] These points are more fully explored in William Niskanen, 'Reflections on Reagonomics', in Boaz (ed.), *op. cit.*, pp. 9-16.

benefits to be derived from being left to make their own economic decisions and, alternatively, from their role in influencing the decisions of government through the various instruments of political participation—voting in elections, lobbying, using the courts, and so on. I could not attempt to offer an answer, and refer the reader to the way in which the question is tackled by Buchanan. He makes a strong case for welcoming the 'new realism' in the Reagan era characterised by the US public's growing disbelief in the ability of governments to identify the constituent parts of 'public interest', far less to know how that interest could best be promoted.

THE LEGACY OF REAGANOMICS

While the evaluation tests listed above are sometimes ambiguous and their interpretation involves subjective judgements, Reaganomics survives these tests surprisingly well in the eyes of both supporters and the more responsible critics. There is, however, a final test which must not be forgotten: In what shape was the economy left on relinquishing office? It is customary for incoming administrations of a different political colour to explain their difficulties in implementing their policies in terms of the 'poor bag of assets' bequeathed to them. It would be difficult for the incoming Bush régime to deploy this argument, even with regard to the failure of Congress to curb the lust of its members for supporting each other's pet spending programmes. As Irwin Stelzer argues, Bush has based his strategy on improving relations with a Congress which is unlikely to stomach further reductions in government regulation of the economy. Democrats are not to be blamed, but to be negotiated with.

Our authors raise two important questions about the legacy of Reaganomics and it is not surprising if they leave them hanging in the air. The first is whether the principles behind getting the government off the backs of the people are sufficiently strong to prevent the electorate being 'still vulnerable to those who promote the competing vision of an expansive state' (Niskanen). One detects a distinct note of pessimism concerning the prospect of constitutional reforms during the Bush administration, including controls on the growth of public spending, which would curb the rapacities of rent-seeking interest groups.

The second question is the more mundane one of how to cope with the legacy of both budget and balance-of-payments deficits. As Patrick

Minford shows, no competing view of the economic theory of public debt would question the need for close co-ordination between fiscal and monetary policy combined with a serious attack on limiting the growth in the budget deficit. But by what means and with what degree of commitment?

Whatever view one takes about the prospects for supply-side economics in influencing US (or for that matter UK) policies, both intellectual thrust and its practical manifestation in the performance of the US and UK economies are having immense influence on economic thinking and practice in both East and West. That may well be identified by the world at large as the most important part of the legacy. Let Irwin Stelzer have the last word: ' . . . Reaganomics and Thatcherism may be about to slow in their respective countries, while it quickens in the rest of the world'.

Edinburgh,
February 1989

ALAN PEACOCK

1

POST-REAGAN POLITICAL ECONOMY

James M. Buchanan

Director, Center for Study of Public Choice,
George Mason University, Fairfax, Virginia

I. INTRODUCTION

I PROPOSE to discuss the post-Reagan political economy of the United States, a subject that surely has some relevance for the political economy of the United Kingdom. It is possible to make some relatively secure predictions about the sort of problems that will arise. The Reagan record has been written, and we can define the 'roads not taken' during eight years with some accuracy. Any discussion of the post-Reagan political economy will necessarily involve an assessment of the Reagan presidency, one that is specifically limited here to the political economy of policy.

My theme is both simple and familiar. I assess the Reagan presidency as one of failed opportunity to secure the structural changes that might have been within the realms of the politically possible. The result is that, after Reagan, the institutions in place will remain roughly the same as those existing in 1980. And the potential for mutual and reciprocal exploitation through the political process, the behavioural domain of those persons and groups (the rent seekers) that seek private gain through the agencies of government, will not have been substantially reduced in range and scope.

On the other hand, the shift in public attitudes that made the

1

Reagan ascendancy possible will not be reversed by a shift in administration. There will be no return to the romantic delusion that the national government offers cures for all problems: real, imagined, evolved, or invented. After Reagan we shall live in a political economy that embodies widespread public scepticism about government's capacities, and also about the purity of the motivations of political agents. But, as noted, at the same time we shall have in place all of the institutional trappings that emerged during the apogee of our romantic interlude with politicisation.

The Struggle Between Interest Groups

Politics involves playing many simultaneous games with and between shifting coalitions of interests. Broadly, however, it is useful to think of politics, post-Reagan, as a struggle between the rent seekers, who try to secure private profits or rents through the authority of government, and the constitutionalists, who seek to constrain this authority. And it is important to recognise that all of us, or almost all, are likely to play on both sides of this super game simultaneously. We behave as rent seekers when we support expanded spending programmes or tax breaks to benefit our own industry, occupation, region, local authority, or, quite simply, our own pet version of some 'public interest'. We shall behave as constitutionalists when we recognise the overreaching of government in general.

This struggle will proceed independently of the particular electoral results of 1988. The apparent competition among and between personalities and parties will matter much less than the struggle within each of us, as citizens, between resort to politics and explicit search for limits on politics. The question is clear: Without the putative legitimacy that was provided by the romantic delusion, can the rent seekers dominate the constitutionalists? Or will the return to some semblance of the 18th-century wisdom about the potential for abuse of political authority generate, in turn, some effective embodiment of the 18th-century limits on this authority?

A Modern Constitutionalism?

In one sense, we may read the Reagan era in the United States as an interlude between the romantic follies represented by Kennedy's Camelot and Johnson's Great Society, and one of the two post-Reagan options that I have suggested. The first post-Reagan scenario involves the raw struggle of interests in majoritarian politics constrained by no constitutional limits; the second post-Reagan scenario could reflect the beginnings of a return to some modern version of the dream of James Madison. And we should make no mistake that one of these two outcomes (or a mixture of the two) must describe post-Reagan political economy. The basic struggle was exemplified in the arguments of the 1988 presidential aspirants, both of whom seemed unwilling to challenge the rent seekers directly while at the same time both seemed to recognise that rent-seeking demands must be constrained.

In Section II, I explain my verdict that the Reagan leadership is one of lost opportunity. In Section III, I shall briefly examine the Reagan fiscal policy agenda, and relate this agenda to more comprehensive issues. In Section IV, I describe the change in perception and consequent evaluation of politics and politicians that has occurred only since the 1960s. In Section V, I discuss the supergame between the rent seekers and the constitutionalists in more detail. And finally, in Section VI, I relate the argument to American constitutional democracy, by comparison and contrast with the parliamentary democracy of the United Kingdom.

II. POLICY WITHIN POLITICS VERSUS STRUCTURAL REFORM

Those who are familiar with my various writings will recognise that it is necessary here to review briefly the methodological perspective of the constitutional economist. Some appreciation of this perspective is required in order to understand my assessment of the Reagan enterprise. There is a categorical distinction to be made between playing the policy game within the rules of ordinary politics and engaging in the wider exercise of considering the rules themselves, by which I mean the institutional/constitutional structure that constrains the workings of politics.

A central objective of the Reagan presidency was to reduce the politicisation of the national economy, to reverse in direction a movement that had been going on for almost a century. In political economy terms, the characteristic feature of this century has been the growth in size and scope of the public sector, along with the increasing concentration of authority in the central or federal government. This feature has not, of course, been unique to the United States. The 20th century has been characterised by the growth of government everywhere.

Fixed Rules or Incentive Structures
There are two ways in which the Reagan objective of reduced politicisation might have been approached. The first, which I have called
'policy within politics', embodies the presumption that the rules, the
institutional-constitutional structure from which political decisions
emerge, are fixed. By inference, the failure of pre-Reagan politics to
have advanced the cause of depoliticisation was attributed to the
presence of the 'wrong' parties and the 'wrong' politicians in positions
of decision-making authority. In this view, the specific task for the
dominant coalition of Reagan supporters was to repeal and reverse
policy steps taken by the pre-Reagan 'socialists' of all stripes.

The constitutional economist, who might have shared the stipulated
objective of depoliticisation, would not have accepted this
interpretation of the Reagan enterprise. His was a totally different
diagnosis of the pre-Reagan political economy. The increasing
politicisation of the national economy over this century was attributed,
not to the preferences of ideologically-driven political coalitions, but to
the incentive structure embedded in the existing institutions from
which political choices emerge. In this approach, it matters relatively
little, if at all, which parties or which politicians succeed or fail in the
overt electoral competition. The constitutional economist would have
based his expectations for any permanent change only in modifications
of the incentive structure.

As might have been anticipated, there were elements of both of
these approaches in the early Reagan rhetoric. There was talk of the
need to change the rules, as well as of the great things to be expected
when the 'other side' was thrown out and 'our men' put in their place.
In 1980 and earlier, Ronald Reagan supported the proposal for a
constitutional amendment to require the federal government to
balance its budget and to impose limits on rates of growth in total
spending. He also promised, in his campaign rhetoric of 1980, to
eliminate the cabinet-level departments of education and energy.

It was evident, however, even before inauguration in January 1981,
that the Reagan leadership was to move primarily if not exclusively
along the policy-within-politics route and to relegate to secondary
status any attempt to achieve genuine structural change. Early
proposals to examine the structure of arrangements for monetary
authority were rejected; the balanced-budget amendment was not
supported during the early months; no mention was made of the
promised elimination of departments. These were opportunities that

were lost by the new administration from the time it took office. The Reagan administration became itself a part of the existing structure; it could no longer succeed in generating changes in the structure itself. All it was left with was to play the standard political game.

III. TAXING, SPENDING, AND DEBT

The stipulated objective of reducing the politicisation of the national economy was widely shared by the American electorate in the 1980s. One measure of the extent of politicisation is the size and rate of increase in the federal government's budget, the total rate of expenditure. There was general support for President Reagan's argument that programme spending was, in general, grossly over-extended and that rates of tax were too high, and had been allowed to increase too rapidly during the inflation of the 1970s.

A meaningful criterion for policy designed to reduce the rate of increase in federal outlay is the present value of anticipated outlay over an indefinite period. A policy designed to reduce rates of increase in current-period outlay only at the cost of ensuring increased rates of spending in later periods would not seem defensible. Yet this short-term policy is precisely the one followed by the Reagan administration. Projected rates of increase in tax revenues were cut in 1981, but *without* correspondingly reduced rates of increase in federal spending. The increased shortfall of revenues behind the increase in outlay was residually financed by the sale of debt, that is, by incurring budget deficits.

The result was that, for the Reagan years, taxpayers had available, for private disposition, an expanded level of purchasing power, relative to that which would have been available under a scenario that matched cuts in rates of increase in taxes and in government spending. This result seems appropriate only if the objective was to give more funds to individuals during the Reagan years, in disregard of the effects in subsequent years. What will be these latter effects, given the policy history sketched out? The outlays during the Reagan years, and before, that were financed by debt must be 'paid for' during the post-Reagan years by service charges represented in interest payments. To the extent that interest charges become a necessary component in the federal budget, these charges will be matched dollar-for-dollar by reductions in funds available for private disposition. The increase in the funds available for private disposition during the Reagan years is precisely matched by the reduction in funds available for private disposition during post-Reagan years. The deficit financing of Reagan-year spending will have accomplished nothing other than a displacement of real cost in time, which is what the classical theory of public debt emphasised.

The Effect of the Budget Deficit

Can the Reagan fiscal policy be defended in terms of the present-value criterion suggested above? Did the residual financing of outlay by debt, with mounting deficits, exert pressures on the Congress to hold down rates of increase in spending more than would have been exerted through tax financing? This argument was, indeed, prominent in the Reagan White House. By forcing a political disequilibrium between the two financing sources, taxes and debt, through the initial 1981 marginal-rate reduction of tax, the politically-supportable rates of spending might have been lower than that rate financed by an equilibrium adjustment between the two financing sources. This argument would, however, seem to fly in the face of more elementary public-choice logic which suggests that political decision-makers, like individuals in their private capacities, will tend to spend more when the borrowing option is present than when it is not. The precise weights to be given to these offsetting arguments cannot be assigned here.

Nevertheless, the legacy of the Reagan fiscal policy is not in dispute. In post-Reagan years, the funds available for private disposition by individuals must be lower than if tax increases had kept pace with increases in expenditure. The costs of spending during the Reagan years will be borne by taxpayers and/or frustrated programme beneficiaries (and holders of government debt instruments if indirect or direct default is considered an option). Rates of tax will be higher and/or rates of spending on public programmes will be lower than they would have been under the alternative financing régime. The commonly observed comment about chickens coming home to roost is appropriate.

How might this result have been avoided if a structural approach to policy had been followed? It seems clear that Reagan's early mandate was sufficient to have secured approval of a constitutional amendment to require budget balance and to impose limits on rates of increase in federal spending. This policy package, with an appropriate phase-in period before balance in the budget was to be achieved, would not have reduced rates of increase in taxes so dramatically as experienced under the Reagan presidency. Rates of outlay might have increased less than those we have observed during these years, although, as I suggested above, this conclusion may be debated by economists using different models. But the important conclusion which cannot be rejected is that, in post-Reagan years, citizens, whether as taxpayers, programme beneficiaries, or creditors, will be worse off than they would have been under the suggested alternative for policy.

IV. POLITICS AND POLITICIANS POST-REAGAN

The fiscal legacy alone places major constraints on the flexibility of response of any political coalition in the post-Reagan years. It will prove difficult to mount support for new programmes of spending, given the size of the budget deficit and the large interest component included in it. The threat or existence of emerging deficits may or may not have constrained rates of spending, relative to those rates that would have been supported under tax financing, in the 1980s. The existence of the accumulated debt, with its accompanying interest charges, must constrain rates of spending in the 1990s. This fiscal constraint may, however, be somewhat unimportant relative to the more principled constraint embodied in the attitude of the citizenry towards politics and politicians.

We can, I think, be assured that there will be no return, post-Reagan, to the romantic illusion that characterised politics during the 1960s. The Reagan presidency represented an anti-politics mentality on the part of the citizenry (the electorate), a mentality that reflected a fundamental shift in public attitudes over the decades of the 1970s and 1980s. It may be useful here to review this dramatic shift in public opinion.

The Growth of Government

I noted earlier that the first two-thirds of this century were characterised by a dramatic growth in the size of the public or governmental sector of the economy, whether this growth be measured by rates of increase in public spending, taxation, regulation or some other broader standard. Such growth rates were not, of course, unique to the USA. Indeed, the UK and other nations of Western Europe experienced even more dramatic increases than the US over the same period. In the USA this politicisation of economic life occurred in several distinct stages. A potted history may be useful.

The 'progressive era' that describes the turn of the century embodied attitudes that were highly critical of the unbridled market economy and offered the arguments for later politicised interferences. The 1913 enactment of the 16th amendment to the US written constitution authorised the levying of a progressive income tax. This amendment was critically important because income tax provided a source of revenue that would grow disproportionately with the growth in national income, either real or nominal. World War I, as all other wars, expanded the central government's authority, and, although there was considerable depoliticisation in the 1920s, the instruments of authority remained in place. Franklin Roosevelt's New Deal, as a response to the economic emergency of the Great Depression, reflected widespread public support for new, expanded, and often ill-conceived, programmes of governmental activity. World War II followed and, once again, the crisis itself facilitated an increase in government's authority.[1]

Eisenhower's 1950s were characterised by much less political retrenchment than the 1920s. The decade of the 1950s in the United States is best described as a holding operation. There followed the bizarre decade of the 1960s, which witnessed the apogee of public support for politicisation at least a decade later than the comparable situation in the UK. The artificial and essentially romantic ideas of Kennedy's Camelot were, however, well on the way to exposure and prospective oblivion when the 1963 assassination of Kennedy and the subsequent ascendancy of Lyndon Johnson provided the impetus required to enact left-over New Deal legislation that was three decades out of date.

The Romantic Delusion

In retrospect, from our vantage point in 1988, it seems amazing that this whole period of dramatic growth in the politicisation of economic life in the USA and elsewhere, occurred in the absence of any plausibly realistic theory of how politics actually works. We were everywhere trapped in the romantic delusion stemming from Hegelian idealism: the state was, somehow, a benevolent entity and those who made decisions on behalf of the state were guided by consideration of the general or public interest. Thus welfare economists considered there

---

[1] Robert Higgs's book, *Crisis and Leviathan*, New York: Oxford University Press, 1986, provides a good source for the material sketched out here.

was a *prima facie* case for politicisation of an activity once the market was judged to have failed to meet the idealised criterion of maximal efficiency.

The set of attitudes which embodies these ideas was shifted in the 1960s and beyond. There are two identifiable reasons for the change. First of all, in the USA, Lyndon Johnson's extensions of the welfare state failed demonstrably in many instances; these failures were directly observed by citizens as well as by research scholars and specialists. The failures were often described in terms of the 'capture' of programmes by special-interest beneficiaries whose motivation seemed to be private and personal gains.

The second identifiable reason for the shift in attitude towards politicisation was the development and promulgation of a theory of how politics actually works, along with accompanying analyses of how politicians actually behave. Public choice theory, broadly defined, came along in the 1960s, 1970s, and 1980s to offer intellectual foundations that allowed citizens to understand the political failures they were able to observe at first hand. This theory, in its simplest terms, does little more than to extend the behavioural model used by economists to choices made by persons in political roles (as voters, politicians, bureaucrats). Once this elementary shift in vision is made, however, the critical flaw in the idealised model of politics and politicians is exposed. No longer could the romanticised model of the workings of the state be tolerated.

Identifying Special Interests

Politics was, for the first time in two centuries, seen as a very complex interaction process, in which many persons, in many roles, seek a whole set of divergent objectives, which include a large measure of their own private economic gains. Politicians in elected office seek re-election, and this dictates that they be responsive to the desires of constituents. And constituents seek to profit from politics just as they seek to profit from their private activities. Politics, as a game among competing special-interest groups, each of which is organised for the pursuit of profit through the arms and agencies of the state, takes on a wholly different colouration in the post-1960s from that which it assumed in the decades before the 1960s.

The reaction on the part of the public was that which might have been anticipated. By the mid-1970s, the rhetoric of anti-politics had entered the political debates. Both the 1976 Carter and, more emphatically, the 1980 Reagan electoral successes stemmed from this shift in public attitudes, as did the 1979 Thatcher victory in the UK. For more than a decade the electorates have viewed politics and politicians more realistically than they have done for more than a century.

I have traced out this history because it is helpful in making projections of the post-Reagan political economy. I should emphasise that there will be no return to the romantic delusion about politics that characterised public and academic attitudes throughout most of this century. The socialist god is emotionally and intellectually dead. Despite the occasional rhetorical flourish from the old left and its political spokesmen, no political leader, post-Reagan in the United States, will have the flexibility that Roosevelt, Kennedy, or Johnson possessed. Political leadership, post-Reagan, and independently of party, must confront a citizenry that will remain sceptical of political nostrums and that will attribute special-interest motivations to any and all political agents. This public scepticism will be added on to the fiscal constraints already noted. The challenge to be faced by any prospective political leader in the post-Reagan years is immense.

V. RENT SEEKERS VERSUS CONSTITUTIONALISTS

I suggested above (p. 2) that the post-Reagan political economy in America will be described by the struggle between the rent seekers and the constitutionalists, and that almost all citizens will play, simultaneously, both of these roles. If we understand modern democratic politics in these terms, we remain within realistic models and steer clear of engaging in romantic images. Each of us will seek to utilise the political process to further the privately determined and specialised interest that affects us most directly, either through providing us with desired, positively valued activities from which we secure benefits or through preventing negatively valued actions from being carried out to our cost. In this use of the political process we are rent seekers, and I use this term to refer to any sought-for objective that involves concentrated benefits or costs.

If I seek a special tax exemption for my industry, my profession, my region, I am rent seeking. If I seek a special spending programme that will benefit my pet project, whether this will provide me with personal pecuniary gain or not, I am rent seeking. I am seeking to secure *differential* gains that are not shared by the full constituency. In game theory terms, I am behaving non-co-operatively; I am engaging in politics treated as a non-co-operative game. To the extent that politics may be accurately regarded as a competitive struggle among the rent seekers, it will, in total, be negative sum, or, at best, zero sum—that is to say, the aggregate losses will be larger than the aggregate gains.

A Negative-Sum Game

If this is all there is to politics, if all, or almost all, members of the polity consider themselves to wind up as net losers, despite the differential gains that may be secured from favourable political action on their favoured programme, pressures will increase to change the rules. Why will rational persons continue to play in a negative-sum game and, further, negative sum over all, or almost all, participants? If this result should be characteristic of a game in which persons voluntarily participate, the game could not survive. Players would, quite simply, leave the game. In this sense, it is improper to model politics by analogy with voluntary games. Individual members of a political community cannot readily exercise an exit option, especially at the level of the national political unit. If emigration thresholds are high, individuals must change the rules as an alternative to leaving the game itself.

In taking action to change the rules of the political game, based on the recognition that the rent-seeking struggle takes place within the existing rules, the individual behaves as a constitutionalist. I have suggested that, within each of us, there is a conflict between our political behaviour as a rent seeker and our political behaviour as a constitutionalist.

Rising Above Interest Groups

In a paper delivered at the American Economic Association meetings in Chicago in December 1987, William Niskanen, former member of Reagan's Council of Economic Advisers, pointed to three separate political events in the United States that seem to reflect the constitutionalist element at work in the political process, the element that is basically co-operative rather than conflictual.[2] He pointed to the whole deregulation movement, to the tax reform legislation of 1986, and to the Gramm-Rudman-Hollings budgetary constraints, enacted

---

[2] William Niskanen, 'The Political Economy of Gramm-Rudman and other "Policy Accidents"' (unpublished manuscript), Washington DC: Cato Institute, 1987.

first in 1985 and revised in 1987. In each of these cases, the beneficiaries seem to be the citizenry generally rather than concentrated interest groups. As Niskanen suggested, the political economist who tries to remain with a rent-seeking model of democratic politics cannot explain these events. These events can be satisfactorily understood only when it is recognised that a constitutionalist model, which directs attention towards effective changes in rules that will benefit all, or almost all, players, also explains at least some aspects of observed political reality.

As I have noted earlier, the distinguishing feature of the post-Reagan political economy will be that the struggle between the rent-seeking special interests and the constitutionalist effort to secure general benefits from changes in rules, will be carried on without the romantic delusion that political agents seek to further some general or 'public interest', or, indeed, that any such interest exists. Before the 1960s, this delusion was omnipresent in all discussions about and attitudes towards politics and politicians. And it was this delusion that enabled many special-interest programmes involving concentrated benefits to be approved unwittingly by the electorate. Because these programmes are now established, as a part of the post-Reagan *status quo*, we cannot predict wholesale dismantling, even if the error in initial politicisation comes to be widely acknowledged. We can, however, predict that, without the romance of the public interest, or of the genuinely benevolent state, special benefits to concentrated interests will be more difficult to implement through the political process. Can we expect to see more Tulsa or Tombigbee canals, both notorious examples of American 'pork-barrel' spending, in the 1990s?

Binding Constraints

Let me be a bit more specific about the supergame involving the rent seekers and the constitutionalists in particular areas of policy and politics. There is perhaps a better recognition of the negative-sum aspects of the spending-taxing-deficit process, as carried on by both the Reagan presidency and the Congress in the 1980s, than for other areas of policy. The Gramm-Rudman-Hollings legislation, although not so desirable from a constitutionalist perspective as an amendment to the United States' written constitution would be, nonetheless reflects a recognition by the Congress that its spending rules, its procedures, were out of hand and that binding constraints are required. The test for the post-Reagan years will be whether or not the discipline signalled by the Gramm-Rudman-Hollings legislation, and by the attempts to work within its discipline, will carry over beyond 1991.

The issue on which there does not seem to be adequate recognition for the necessity to operate within general rules that constrain political rent seeking is that of trade policy. Potentially, the post-Reagan political economy seems most vulnerable to the protectionist urgings of special-interest groups which may, through a set of logrolled political exchanges, succeed in imposing major damage on the national economy. We could find our incomes reduced in post-Reagan years if we allow legislation to be enacted that will close up our markets. This threat can be contained and offset only if the citizenry, and its political agents, recognise the self-defeating or negative-sum aspect of the protectionist argument. The constitutionalist position here is that which was taken by Cordell Hull in the 1930s; trade policy, industry-by-industry, cannot effectively be made by Congress, which necessarily allows for complex trade-offs among separate beneficiary groups to the damage of the general electorate.

VI. CONSTITUTIONAL DEMOCRACY

Any description of the American political economy, post-Reagan, must be informed by an understanding of what the American polity is and how it differs from other national polities. The United States is a republic; there is a written constitution, a two-house legislature, an executive with veto powers, and a supreme court with authority for review. This political régime is different in many respects from the idealised parliamentary democracy, which is much closer to the majoritarian model of collective decision-making so favoured by political scientists. Majority coalitions in the USA are much more constrained in what they can do and the speed with which they can do it than are parliamentary régimes. This difference alone is, I think, sufficient to explain why the American economy came to be somewhat *less* politicised over the century when politics was viewed romantically than those other Western economies, including the United Kingdom, where majoritarian dominance was characteristic. But this difference also explains why Mrs Thatcher has been more successful than Ronald Reagan in carrying through on pledges and promises for effective depoliticisation. Parliamentary régimes depend relatively more on who is in office and relatively less on the incentive structure facing whoever is in elective office. Put very simply, a constitutional democracy is constitutional, which means that rules matter.

The President's Opportunity

This difference in structure is important in understanding my overall theme for this paper. Let me return to the supergame involving rent-seeking competition on the one hand and constitutional efforts to change the rules on the other. By the nature of the structure, special-interest coalitions tend to find their initial support in the US Congress, which is organised, deliberately, on the basis of dispersed geographic representation. Congressional dominance of the executive necessarily implies that relatively more political rent seeking will take place with relatively less constitutional thrust. By contrast, because the President is representative of the whole electorate, there is, in the presidency, a 'natural' location for attention to genuinely constitutional approaches to policy reform. It is in this sense that I judge the Reagan presidency to have failed; it paid too little attention to structure and it seems to have been too interested in playing the policy-within-politics game, too interested in pushing its policy agenda within a relatively short time perspective.

What can we predict for post-Reagan politics? Quite independently of the electoral results, because of the constitutional structure itself we can predict reasonable stability in policy. There can be no dramatic reversals in trend. Indeed, 1933 was perhaps unique to US history in that this was a peacetime year when dramatic change was possible. A post-Reagan president can adopt a constitutionalist stance and consider proposing changes in the rules that will effectively constrain the rent seekers. The opportunity for this position to be successful will not, however, be that faced by Ronald Reagan in 1980. Quite apart from prospects for success, there seems little likelihood that the new President will adopt even so partial a constitutionalist stance as Reagan did in 1980. If policy-within-politics ultimately came to dominate the Reagan years, we can scarcely expect the post-Reagan president to place structural change high on his attention listing.

Mutual Exploitation or Rule Change

Hard-headed and sober predictions about the post-Reagan years suggest that we will witness relatively more negative-sum rent seeking through the agencies of national politics. These predictions are tempered somewhat when we recognise the total absence of any supportive romantic image of governmental benevolence. Can the rent seekers continue to engage in mutual exploitation through politics without some myth of public interest? My own romantic prediction, based largely on hope rather than analysis, is that the time will be ripe for intellectual entrepreneurs in particular to convey the constitutionalist message. This message is simple and does not urge persons to act contrary to their interests. Changing the rules can be, and is, in the interests of *all* the players, especially as they are caught up in the competitive struggle among interest groups, each of which exploits all others. Personally, I think I have a moral obligation to believe that we can move towards a restoration of the vision of James Madison.

POST-ELECTION POSTSCRIPT

The substantial election victory of George Bush confirms my hypothesis that the romance between the American electorate and the state has faded into near-oblivion. Even if somewhat lukewarmly proffered, Governor Dukakis did call for an extension and expansion of the political domain of the federal government. The accompanying electoral successes of the Democrats in both houses of the Congress confirmed another hypothesis concerning the increasing importance of rent-seeking, special-interest politics. Members of Congress act in furtherance of the interests of defined constituencies, and one of President Bush's major problems will be to control the excesses that coalitions of special-interest groups will seek to enact.

Protectionist legislation, additional to that which is already embodied in the 1988 trade bill, will move through the Congress. George Bush and James Baker seem to understand the logic of free trade, but whether their expected rhetoric will be matched by effective control of protectionist pressures is not predictable. More generally, there is no indication that George Bush thinks and acts on the basis of *constitutional principle* even to the extent that motivated Ronald Reagan.

Bush deliberately locked himself into a no-tax-increase position in his campaign commitments. He will succeed in holding off tax-rate increases if costs under Medicare can be reasonably contained, and if new spending initiatives are kept in check. The payroll tax increases enacted in 1983 are beginning to accumulate surpluses in the social security account, and these surpluses act to make the budget deficit, overall, seem less than independent accounting would suggest. The

Gramm-Rudman targets for reduction in the size of the comprehensive deficit can be met under favourable economic conditions, even if the problems of funding future commitments to retirees are exacerbated.

The most severe threat to economic policy in the Bush presidency may stem from a possible financial crisis, triggered by collapse of saving and loan units, or by foreign debtors. If, in response to such crises, the Federal Reserve authority responds with increases in liquidity, inflationary pressures will accelerate, with rapidly shifting expectations. This inflation would, in turn, prompt monetary restrictions which would generate recession. This scenario need not occur, but the fragility, and hence non-predictability, of the whole set of complex monetary arrangements, both domestic and international, ought to be emphasised.

There is little or no evidence that a Bush-Baker-Brady administration will understand or seek *constitutional* approaches to the resolution of the issues of political economy that must surely emerge in the 1989-93 years.

2

REAGANOMICS: A BALANCED ASSESSMENT

William A. Niskanen

Chairman of the Cato Institute, Washington DC

ANY EVALUATION of the Reagan record will depend on the standards by which it is judged. I will evaluate the Reagan economic record by two standards: the performance of the Carter administration and Reagan's initial objectives. In most dimensions, the economic record of the Reagan administration was clearly superior to that of the Carter administration, and that is the basis for the continued popular support of this record. In terms of his own objectives, Reagan did not accomplish as much as he first proposed, and that is the basis for the disappointment of his strongest supporters.

Reaganomics was the most ambitious attempt to change the course of American economic policy by any administration since the New Deal. Moreover, Reagan, unlike Franklin Roosevelt, told us about most of his programmes during his first campaign. The consistent and distinct theme of this programme, in Reagan's words, was that 'only by reducing the growth of government can we increase the growth of the economy'. The four key elements of this programme were to

o   reduce the growth of federal spending;

o   reduce individual and corporate tax rates;

o   reduce federal regulation; and,

o   reduce inflation by monetary restraint.

17

Delivering the Promises

In direction, if not in magnitude, Reagan delivered on each of these promises.

The annual growth of real federal spending was reduced from 4 per cent during the Carter administration to less than 3 per cent during the Reagan administration, despite a record peacetime increase in military spending. Individual and corporate tax rates were reduced more than anyone initially anticipated. Some further deregulation followed the considerable deregulation approved late in the Carter administration. And the inflation rate was reduced more rapidly than anyone initially anticipated. Moreover, among the more important developments were the dogs that did not bark. The Reagan administration was the first in two decades that did not impose some form of general price and wage controls. And until 1987, few new programmes were proposed that would increase the budget in future years. One of the more enduring achievements was the appointment of a large number of federal judges who are more supportive of the basic economic rights enshrined in our Constitution.

General economic conditions are also quite favourable. The current recovery was by December 1988 in its 73rd month, the longest peacetime recovery in US history. During this recovery, the US economy generated over 18 million additional jobs, with especially high employment growth for young people, minorities, and women. The unemployment rate is now the lowest for 14 years. This condition is the envy of the world, especially in Europe where total employment has been stagnant for two decades. The growth of productivity and real earnings is still low, but has increased relative to the dismal record during the Carter administration. Productivity growth has been especially high in those industries most subject to foreign competition— agriculture, manufacturing and mining. The growth of real earnings has been highest for women, especially 'minority' women. Since the end of the Carter administration, both the rate of inflation and long-term interest rates have declined about 6 percentage points. Moreover, in the absence of a major policy mistake, there is no reason to expect a recession in the near future.

This is a substantial record, for which Reagan deserves credit. It is implausible to believe that President Carter or whoever else might have been elected in 1984 could have accomplished as much. Reagan is already regarded as one of the several most effective presidents in the post-war years.

No Reagan Revolution

In the end, however, there was no Reagan revolution. Although the growth of federal spending was reduced, the federal budget share of GNP, until recently, continued to increase. Although individual and corporate tax rates were reduced by more than anyone anticipated, some of the reduction in tax rates was financed by shifting taxes to the future (via the deficit), or by increasing the taxes on new investment. Some deregulation was offset by a net increase in trade restraints. Moreover, the failure to reform the remaining governmental role in several industries left a legacy of a high rate of bank failures, a large future bill to close those banks that are insolvent but still operating, increasing air traffic congestion, and the prospect of some re-regulation.

Although inflation was reduced more rapidly than anyone anticipated, there is still no consensus on a rule for the conduct of monetary policy. And although the economic recovery has been sustained longer than usual, average economic growth in the 1980s has been about the same as in the 1970s. A Reagan revolution would have reduced the number of lawyers in active practice and reduced the price of real estate in Washington; I need not remind you of what happened!

In the absence of any significant change in the institutions, incentives and constraints on federal policies, the substantial achievements of Reaganomics could be reversed in one term of the Bush administration, although this is not likely. The future of Reaganomics will depend critically on how its major adverse legacy— the large federal deficit—is resolved. Only sustained budget restraint can sustain the major achievements of Reaganomics. The normal problem of constraining the growth of government spending will be compounded by the bills now becoming due for a number of very expensive weapons systems, the closure of insolvent banks, and for repairing and replacing the government's nuclear materials facilities. A policy to reduce the deficit by either tax-rate increase or by re-inflation, however, would reverse these major achievements.

Supply-Side Survival

How much of Reaganomics will survive? On this issue, I am moderately optimistic. The substantial reduction in marginal tax rates has become the symbol of tax reform, both in the United States and abroad, and is unlikely to be reversed. House Speaker Jim Wright's proposal to maintain the higher 1987 rates was rebuffed by his own party. Mr Bush made an unusually strong commitment against any tax increase, and he proposed several selective reductions in tax rates and the tax base. Although Bush may later acquiesce to some minor tax increases, few people propose or expect any increase in individual or corporate tax rates. The basic contribution of 'supply-side' economics will, I believe, survive, long after this phrase disappears from political discourse.

Similarly, the substantial reduction in inflation is not likely to be reversed. During the 1970s, politicians in many countries claimed that rising inflation was out of their control, at various times blaming inflation on OPEC, the weather, greedy businesses or unions, or whatever other external condition provided some temporarily plausible explanation. The substantial reduction in inflation in most of the advanced countries during the 1980s, however, demonstrated that inflation is primarily a monetary phenomenon and can be reduced, albeit at some temporary cost, by sustained monetary restraint. This will make it more difficult for politicians to re-inflate, again long after the term 'monetarism' disappears from political discourse.

The primary remaining problem is that there is no consensus on a rule for the conduct of monetary policy. More specifically, we expect our central banks to do too much: at various times to sustain the recovery, reduce inflation, stabilise exchange rates, or whatever is perceived to be the most important problem of the moment. My primary immediate concern is that the major central banks will take the Louvre Agreement on exchange rates too seriously, increasing the instability of domestic demand in an attempt to reduce the instability of exchange rates. My primary longer-term concern is that we have delegated one of the most important governmental roles to the discretion of our unelected central bankers, however intelligent and well-intentioned, without a clear, sustainable rule for the conduct of monetary policy.

The Future of Reaganomics

On other issues, the future of Reaganomics is much less clear. Mr Bush has proposed increased spending for education and the environment and a variety of small tax preferences that will reduce the revenue base. Moreover, he will probably be forced to approve some part of the agenda of the congressional Democrats as the price for congressional approval of administration initiatives. The still-large federal deficit will constrain new proposals for spending increases or tax cuts but is likely to divert the demands for special benefits into mandates on employers, selective trade restraints, and other forms of regulation. Although the Bush victory was based on the Reagan record, Mr Bush and his associates are much less ideological, much more receptive to consider federal responses to almost any perceived problem. One of the ironies of the Reagan record is that he restored the perception that the federal government could be effective, a perception that also serves those with a very different agenda.

The major domestic opportunity of the Bush administration will be to consolidate the Reagan economic programme. The major risk is a continued stalemate, similar to the last two years of the Reagan administration. Although Mr Bush won by a substantial margin, his victory had no coattails and an ambiguous mandate. The Democrats, with a quite different agenda, increased their margin in both Congress and the States. And some residual bitterness about the Bush campaign may have reduced the potential for bipartisan co-operation in the national interest. In effect, Mr Bush will have to prove his own mandate by forceful early actions and some early successes. Otherwise, the Bush administration may turn out like the Ford administration, but without Ford's forceful veto record. A stalemate may not be the worst possible outcome, but it would be a sad commentary on the capacity of our political system to resolve problems and pursue opportunities that serve our shared interests.

In retrospect, there was little reason to expect a Reagan revolution. As candidate and president, Reagan endorsed the major surviving programmes of the New Deal and the post-war consensus on foreign policy and defence. Most of the initial Reagan programme represented a rather cautious evolution of policies supported by a broad bipartisan consensus beginning in the late 1970s. One does not achieve a revolution by appointing known advocates of the conventional wisdom to head several domestic departments. A revolutionary president would have appointed competent revolutionaries, not the mediocre crowd of 'horseholders' from California. One might expect better managers, so that the huge increase in federal spending on agriculture, defence and medical care generated more demonstrable benefits. One might hope for a chief of staff to maximise the President's policy agenda, rather than the President's personal popularity. A different set of appointments and a different political strategy would have been more controversial but would probably have added to Reagan's considerable achievements.

A Change in Perceptions

The primary reason why Reaganomics did not prove to be a revolution, however, is that there has not yet been a fundamental change in the perceptions about what the federal government should and, more importantly, should not do, at least among elected officials. Ronald Reagan offered a vision that represents the best of our heritage: an America of opportunity, tolerance and caring. His reluctance to face hard choices, however, left some major new problems and an electorate that is still vulnerable to those who promote the competing vision of an expansive state. The most distinctive characteristic of this century has been the pervasive growth of government. Reaganomics may prove to be only a temporary pause in this progressive loss of liberties. A more general sense of outrage about the contemporary role of government, one or more constitutional amendments, and new leaders who share Reagan's vision are probably necessary to protect and extend history's most noble experiment: the American revolution.

3

SUPPLY-SIDE ECONOMICS:
An Assessment of the Theory and Results of American Experience in the 1980s

Paul Craig Roberts

William E. Simon Professor of Political Economy,
Center for Strategic & International Studies,
Washington DC

I. INTRODUCTION

WHEN JOHN F. KENNEDY was elected President of the United States in 1960, Keynesian demand management entered its American heyday. Keynesianism had been entrenched in the universities for a decade or more, and a generation of journalists and civil servants had been inculcated in its principles. There were few critics, and no one paid them any attention. Demand management had free rein and rode off into stagflation and political destruction during the administration of President Jimmy Carter.

Two decades later when Ronald Reagan was elected President, another fiscal revolution occurred, but this time few people and practically no academics were familiar with the supply-side principles at its core. It was a policy born in the congressional budget process and frustrations with stagflation and worsening trade-offs between inflation and unemployment. In the autumn of 1978 the Democratic Congress passed what was later known as Reaganomics—tax-rate reductions combined with reductions in the growth of federal spending—but the measure was killed off by President Carter's announcement that he would veto it. Nevertheless, the Congress rejected the Carter administration's tax reform legislation, designed to close 'loopholes' without lowering tax rates, and cut the capital gains tax rate. The supply-side revolution had begun.

In its 1979 *Annual Report* and again in 1980, the Joint Economic Committee of Congress called for the implementation of a supply-side fiscal policy. During the 1980 presidential campaign the Senate Finance Committee endorsed a supply-side tax cut. The Democrats in the Senate wanted to be identified with the new policy. However, they refrained from passing the tax cut before the presidential election, because it would appear to be an endorsement of Republican Ronald Reagan over their own candidate. The Senate leadership decided to wait until after the November election to pass the tax cut. Unexpectedly, Reagan's victory also cost the Democrats control of the Senate, and the tax-cut issue was delivered firmly into Republican hands.

Supply-Side Politics

The Reagan White House was staffed with people who were unfamiliar with the change in economic thinking that Congress had undergone in the previous four years. Gratuitously uninformed and confident from control of the Senate, the White House staff manoeuvred to deny congressional Democrats any credit for the 1981 tax-rate reduction. When Democrats in the House of Representatives saw that they were being denied a part in the historic legislation in order to give President Reagan a political 'victory', they devised their own tax cut. It was just as supply-side in content as the administration's. Indeed, there was no way to differentiate the two bills politically until Reagan decided to add the indexation of the personal income tax (beginning in 1985) to his measure.

While White House political neophytes were threatening the new policy by denying the Democrats any credit, conservatives, who wanted a rapid victory over inflation at any cost, permitted a disastrous monetary policy during 1981-82. Encouraged by political conservatives, the New York bond houses, and its own fears over inflation, the Federal Reserve inflicted the severest recession in the post-war era. These two errors combined to create a political problem for Reagan. He had picked a fight with Democrats over an issue they were willing to support and claimed a victory over them just as the economy entered deep recession. The Democrats and their allies in the media were quick to take revenge, and budget deficits resulting from the recession were blamed on Reagan's tax cut before the rate reductions were even phased in. By January 1982 large deficits were being attributed to Reagan's supply-side policy even though the first significant cut in taxes was not effective until July 1982 and the second cut was not scheduled until July 1983.

Caricaturing Supply-Side Economics

The lack of understanding outside the Congress of the nature of the new policy allowed both opponents and proponents of supply-side economics to caricature it, often ruthlessly, as the belief that across-the-board tax-rate reductions are self-financing. Today the policy is widely misunderstood as the belief that tax cuts pay for themselves in increased revenues. This misunderstanding has made it easy for the budget deficits to be blamed on the 1981 tax-rate reduction.

The purpose of this paper is to explain concisely and accurately the analytical and empirical bases of the new fiscal policy and to use freely available official statistics to correct widespread misconceptions of the impact the supply-side policy has had on the US economy. Reaganomics was more than tax reductions and fiscal policy. It also comprised a monetarist policy and a policy of economic deregulation. This study does not deal with the regulatory aspects of Reaganomics, and the discussion of monetary policy is limited to its relationship to the 'twin deficits'.

Some of the striking results of Reaganomics were not anticipated. For example, the extraordinary increase in wealth that resulted from the sharp rise in stock and bond prices was not generally expected, because most financial market gurus predicted that inflationary fears would keep the financial markets in the doldrums. The rise in the dollar and the currency's prolonged strength was not anticipated by forecasters for basically the same reason. In 1981 the economics profession interpreted supply-side economics as an inflationary policy. The Federal Reserve was advised by its consultants that monetary policy was the junior partner, a 'weak sister' that would be overwhelmed by expansionist fiscal policy—predictions which reflected economists' lack of knowledge of the basis and origin of the new fiscal policy as well as a firm belief in the 'Phillips curve'.

II. THEORY OF SUPPLY-SIDE ECONOMICS

In the USA in the 1980s, a second post-war fiscal revolution occurred. Keynesian demand management of the economy was replaced by supply-side economics—a policy that focusses on individual incentives. This change represents a fundamental shift in thinking about fiscal policy. In the Keynesian approach, a fiscal change operates to alter demand in the economy. A tax-rate reduction, for example, raises the disposable income of consumers, who then spend more. With government spending held constant, increased consumer spending stimulates supply and moves the economy to higher levels of employment and GNP. In this view, the size of the deficit determines the amount of the stimulus.

In contrast, supply-side economics emphasises that fiscal policy works by changing relative prices or incentives. High income tax rates and regulation are seen as disincentives to work and production regardless of the level of demand. To understand the difference in emphasis between Keynesianism and supply-side economics, consider the removal of a tariff that is high enough to prevent trade in a commodity. When the tariff is repealed, no revenues are lost, no budget deficits result and no money is put into anyone's hands. Yet clearly economic activity will expand, because the disincentive has been removed. Nothing in demand management captures this effect.

Supply-side economics brought a new perspective to fiscal policy by focussing on the relative price effects. Lower tax rates encourage saving, investing, working, and risk-taking. As people switch into these activities out of leisure, consumption, tax shelters and working for non-taxable income, the incentive effects cause an increase in the market supply of goods and services—hence the term 'supply-side economics'. As people respond to the higher after-tax income and wealth, or greater profitability, incomes rise and the tax base grows, thus feeding back some of the lost revenues to the Treasury. The savings rate also rises, providing more funds for government and private borrowing.

Relative-Price Effects of Fiscal Policy

The relative-price argument is straightforward. There are two important relative prices. One governs people's decisions about how they allocate their income between consumption and saving. The cost to the individual of allocating a dollar of income to current consumption is the future income stream given up by not saving and investing that dollar. The present value of that income stream is influenced by marginal tax rates. The higher the marginal rate, the lower is the value of the income stream. High tax rates make consumption cheap in terms of foregone income, and the saving rate declines, resulting in less investment.

The other important relative price governs people's decisions about how they allocate their time between work and leisure or between leisure and improving their education and skills. The cost to a person of allocating additional time to leisure is the current earnings given up by not working (for example, overtime on Saturdays) or the future income given up by not taking courses to improve skills. The value of the foregone income is determined by the rate at which additional income is taxed. The higher the marginal tax rates, the cheaper the price of leisure. Absenteeism goes up, willingness to accept overtime declines, and people spend less time improving their work skills.

Physicians who encountered a 50 per cent tax rate after six months of work were faced with working another six months for only 50 per cent of their actual earnings. Such a low reward for effort encouraged doctors to share practices in order to reduce their working hours and enjoy longer vacations. The high tax rates shrunk the tax base by discouraging physicians from earning additional amounts of taxable income. The high tax rates also drove up the cost of medical care by reducing the supply of medical services.

The effect of tax rates on the decision to earn additional taxable income is not limited to physicians in the top bracket. Studies by Martin Feldstein at the National Bureau of Economic Research found that in many cases the tax rates on the average worker left almost no gap between take-home pay and unemployment compensation. Feldstein found that a 30 per cent marginal tax rate made unemployment sufficiently competitive with work to raise the unemployment rate by 1·25 percentage points and to shrink the tax base by the lost production of one million workers. Blue-collar professionals also encounter disincentive effects even at 'moderate' tax rates. Take the case of a carpenter facing a 25 per cent marginal tax rate. For every additional $100 he earns, he is allowed to keep $75. Suppose his house needs painting and he can hire a painter for $80 a day. Since the carpenter's take-home pay is only $75, he would save $5 by painting his own house. In this case the tax base shrinks by $180—$100 that the carpenter chooses not to earn and $80 that he does not pay the painter.

Studies by Professor Gary Becker of the University of Chicago have shown that capital and labour are employed by households to produce goods and services through non-market activities—for example, the carpenter paints his own house. Goods and services produced in this way are not subject to taxation. The amount of capital and labour that households supply in the market is, therefore, influenced by marginal tax rates. The higher the tax rates, the more likely it is that people can increase their income by using their resources in non-market activities or in the 'black' economy. A clear implication of household economics is that marginal tax rates influence the amount of labour and capital that is used to produce taxable income.

The progressive income tax was devised to 'soak the rich'. In practice it works as a barrier to upward mobility and discourages people from making their best effort. As a result, the tax system can make it more difficult for the average taxpayer to achieve financial independence. It is this barrier to success that supply-side economists attacked. The greater the extent of private success, the smaller the necessity for public assistance and the lower the burden of government. Supply-side economics is not anti-government. It simply accepts the fact that government is costly by nature and maintains that the greater the incentives and opportunities to earn income, the smaller will be the size and burden of government.

Impact of Interest Rates and Taxation on Cost of Capital

Supply-side economics has also brought a new perspective to the impact of interest rates and taxation on the cost of capital. Traditionally, interest rates have been stressed as the important factor in the cost of capital. According to this perspective, higher government revenue from increased taxation can spur capital investment by lowering deficits and interest rates or by building budget surpluses and retiring debt. Recent studies, however, have found taxation to be a major factor in the cost of capital (Roberts *et al.*, 1985, 1986a, 1986b, and 1986c). As taxation also reduces investment, the only certain way to reduce 'crowding out' is to cut government expenditure.

Some economists argued that the real tax burden is measured by the total amount of resources the government removes from the private sector by taxing and borrowing. They therefore argued that a tax cut that is not matched dollar for dollar by a spending cut simply means the government takes by borrowing what it formerly took by taxing.

The total resources claimed by government is a better measure of the tax burden than tax revenues alone. But this adding up of concrete resources can make us blind to another measure of the real tax burden —*the production that is lost to disincentives*. It is difficult to see the production that does not take place because the government has made it unprofitable, but it is nevertheless a part of the tax burden.

From the viewpoint of this more complete measure of the tax burden, a tax cut can be real even if it is not matched dollar for dollar by a spending cut, because a reduction in marginal tax rates changes relative prices and causes people to shift into work out of leisure and into investment out of current consumption. These shifts will occur even if people expect that in the future taxes might be raised to pay off any government debt incurred by cutting tax rates. In the meantime, however, the additional work and investment expands the tax base; to make good on the deficit, future tax rates would not have to be raised as much as they were cut. Moreover, if the government did need more tax revenues in the future to pay off debts, it could raise them by some other type of tax, such as a consumption tax, which does not have the disincentive effects of high marginal income tax rates.

The importance of supply-side economics lies in its claim that fiscal policy works through relative price changes or incentives. This claim is not an assertion of the 'Laffer curve'.

Keynesian Criticism

Keynesians objected to the fiscal emphasis on relative price effects (Roberts, 1984). They argued that the elasticities of response of work and saving to tax rates were zero or negative, and they questioned whether incentive effects would deal effectively with an immediate economic stabilisation problem. Neither objection withstood analysis.

The long run consists of a series of short runs. If policies that are effective over a longer period are neglected because they do not have an immediate impact, and if policies that are damaging over the longer period are adopted because they initially have beneficial results, then policy-makers will inevitably find that they have no solution to the crisis they have provoked. In the USA this happened during the period of stagflation in the mid-1970s.

Some Keynesians argued that the incentive effect of lower tax rates would be perverse. It would let people reach their targeted levels of income sooner and, therefore, they would work less. This could be true for individuals but not in the aggregate. If everyone responded to a tax cut by working less, total production would fall and people would not be able to maintain their living standard while working less. The argument that people would take their tax cut in the form of increased leisure undercut the Keynesian interpretation of expansionary fiscal policy just as thoroughly as it undercut the supply-side interpretation that was its target. When Keynesians realised this, they abandoned this argument. The argument that incentive effects are perverse in the aggregate failed, because it was an attempt to aggregate a series of partial equilibrium analyses (individual responses to a change in relative prices) while ignoring the general equilibrium effects.

Confused thinking on incentives

Today many economists claim that their analysis always incorporated supply-side effects and that they were only opposed to an alleged claim that the 1981 tax-rate reduction would pay for itself. In fact, a decade ago practically every economist was arguing that people responded to incentives in perverse ways. They argued that people have a targeted level of income regardless of the cost of acquiring it, so that a tax cut would allow them to reach their target net income by working less. Lester Thurow, now a dean at Massachusetts Institute of Technology (MIT), actually employed this reasoning to argue for a wealth tax. According to Thurow, a wealth tax is a costless way to raise revenue, because the 'income effect' runs counter to, and dominates, the 'substitution effect'. Therefore, it will cause people to work harder in order to maintain their desired post-tax wealth. Such confused thinking was responsible for the neglect of the relative-price effects of fiscal policy in post-war economic management.

Economists were slow to see the flaw in the argument against incentives. Take something simple, like an assertion that a fixed work-week precludes adjustment of the labour supply to tax-rate changes. This sounded reasonable enough to many who did not realise that the 'adjustments' were reflected in the quality and intensity of work. Thus higher absenteeism and labour turnover, longer average duration of unemployment, and labour demands for shorter work-weeks and more paid vacation were all responses to high marginal tax rates on wages and salaries.

The Keynesian concept of the economy as an unstable private sector that had to be stabilised by fiscal and monetary policies served as a pretext for the expansion of government. It also served the interests of economists by transforming them from ivory-tower denizens to public-spirited social activists, a transformation which increased their power and enlivened their life styles. Unemployment can always be said to be 'too high'. And the rate of economic growth can always be judged to be below 'potential'. Before the supply-side challenge to the Keynesian policy-makers, there was always a 'scientific'. economic reason for expanding government spending programmes that enlarged the constituencies of the Congress and the Federal bureaucracy at the expense of private property rights and economic freedom.

III. SOME EMPIRICAL STUDIES OF THE RELATIVE-PRICE EFFECTS OF FISCAL POLICY

A number of economists have assessed the responsiveness of saving, labour force, and tax revenues to changes in tax rates. The following is a brief summary of empirical studies that have found the responses to be significant.

Saving

The 1964 Kennedy income tax reductions were intended to increase aggregate demand by stimulating consumption leading to additional employment and output. Marginal tax rates were cut by approximately 20 per cent for each bracket, and corporate tax rates were cut by 10 per cent. Popular economics textbooks have reinforced the view that the tax cuts increased demand and propelled a recovery. However, studies by Paul Evans (1981) and the US Treasury (Roberts, 1984) have found that the recovery occurred despite a fall in the propensity to consume. The evidence shows that after the marginal tax-rate reduction went into effect, people spent a smaller percentage of their income. In 1964, actual consumer expenditures dipped below the trend rate. By 1967, consumption was at least $17·5 billion below the previous trend—a sum larger than the size of the personal tax cut (measured in constant dollars).

People were actually consuming a smaller percentage of their income and saving a larger percentage after the tax-rate reduction than before. Following the tax reduction there was a significant increase in the real volume of personal saving, and the personal saving rate rose sharply, reversing the decline begun in the 1960s. The personal saving rate remained high for nearly a decade until demographic changes and rising marginal tax rates pushed it down.

Tax-rate cuts benefit savings

In 1964 real personal saving rose by $6·6 billion above the trend projected prior to the reduction in marginal tax rates. The gain in saving was 74 per cent of the tax cut. In the next two years saving increased by $10·2 billion and $10·8 billion above the previous trend, a gain equal to 72 per cent of the tax cut. In 1967 saving was $19 billion above the previous trend—a gain equal to 121 per cent of the size of the tax cut.

This increase in saving released resources from consumption, thus allowing a rapid growth in business investment. In real terms, capital spending (for both the expansion of the capital stock and the replacement of worn-out stock) had grown at an annual rate of 3·1 per cent during the 1950s and early 1960s through 1962. The remainder of the 1960s saw real capital spending rise over twice as fast, increasing by 6·8 per cent annually. The rate of growth from 1963 to 1966 was especially marked. While growth was high in the corporate sector, small business investment showed the biggest improvements.

The acceleration of investment greatly enhanced the economy's ability to produce. The net stock of capital had grown by 3·5 per cent annually between 1949 and 1963, but with the tax cuts it rose to a 5·0 per cent growth rate for the remainder of the decade. Keynesian economists claim that the investment boom resulted from the investment tax credit passed in 1962, which allowed businesses a direct deduction from their taxes for certain investments. However, the sharp rise in investment could not have taken place if consumers had not released resources from consumption by saving a larger share of their incomes.

Professor Michael Boskin of Stanford University (1978) found that the total elasticity of saving (income and substitution effects combined) was positive at around 0·3 to 0·4. While the size of this response has since been disputed by other studies, Boskin's elasticities are commonly used in econometric studies. Boskin predicted that raising the after-tax rate of return to saving would 'increase income substantially' and 'remove an enormous dead-weight loss to society resulting from the distortion of the consumption-saving choice'.

Another interesting conclusion of Boskin's study is that people will not only respond positively to changes in the relative price of saving or lower tax rates, but also that a larger share of total income will be transferred from capital to labour. Boskin confirms earlier studies indicating that the elasticity of substitution between capital and labour is less than one, so that an increase in the capital-labour ratio (following an increase in saving) leads to a corresponding increase in labour's share of total income. Boskin wrote that:

'the current tax treatment of income from capital induces an astounding loss in welfare due to the distortion of the consumption/saving choice. . . .

Reducing taxes on interest income would in the long run raise the level of income and transfer a substantial portion of capital's share of gross income to labour'.

Lower tax rates raise return on saving and help cash flow

Allen Sinai, Andrew Lin and Russell Robins (1983) examined the 1981 tax-rate reduction. They found that private saving was influenced by the greater rate of return allowed by lower tax rates and that the economy would have performed much more poorly in 1981-82 had it not been for the 1981 tax-rate reduction. They also found that the cash-flow effects of the tax cuts reduced the burden of loan repayment and interest charges on debt, thereby strengthening personal and business balance sheets.

Using an augmented Data Resources model of the US economy incorporating previously neglected effects of after-tax interest rates on saving, investment, and consumption, Sinai *et al.* estimated that the net tax reductions introduced by the Reagan administration increased business saving by $27 billion during 1981-82 and that personal saving rose by $48 billion above the baseline trend in 1982. Sinai *et al.* concluded that in the absence of the tax cut, 'the US economy would have performed considerably worse in 1981 and 1982 than actually was the case', with an additional loss in real GNP of about 1·6 percentage points. 'The evidence indicates that ERTA (the Economic Recovery Tax Act of 1981) has had major impact on US economic growth'.

Effects on Revenues

Dr Lawrence Lindsey (1986) of Harvard University has examined the revenue effects of capital gains taxation. Because capital gains are only taxed when an asset is sold, inclusion of gains in taxable income is largely discretionary from the point of view of the taxpayer. Consequently, tax-rate sensitivity is greater for capital gains income than for other types of income. Lindsey studied the evidence in tax returns from 1965-82. He concludes that capital gains tax revenues are maximised at 20 per cent or lower, 'with a central estimate of 16 per cent'. In response to the Tax Reform Act of 1986 in which capital gains are treated as ordinary income (except in 1987, when the tax rate on capital gains is limited to 28 per cent), Lindsey estimates that taxpayers will respond to the higher tax rates by postponing—in some cases indefinitely—their sales of appreciated assets.

Lindsey (1988) has also researched the revenue effects of lowering the top tax rate from 70 per cent to 50 per cent. He found that taxpayers earning over $200,000 per year paid $18·3 billion more in taxes under the new tax code with a top tax rate of 50 per cent than they would have been expected to pay under the old rates of up to 70 per cent. He continues:

> 'The evidence also indicates that upper-middle-income groups may have increased their labour supply dramatically as a result of the tax-rate reductions, particularly the labour supply of the secondary earner in the family'.

Lindsey estimates that 'by 1985 the 1981 tax cuts had boosted real economic activity (GNP) by about 2 per cent above what it would have been otherwise', and states that 'the equivalent of 2·5 million more people are working today as a result of the supply-side effects of the tax cuts'. He concludes, 'the evidence from a wide range of studies shows that taxpayers are highly sensitive to tax rates in many of their economic activities'.

A US Treasury Department study conducted by Michael Darby (1988) found that the 1978 and 1981 cuts in the capital gains tax rate raised revenue by $15 billion by the end of 1985. The study also concluded that the evidence suggested that a capital gains rate reduction 'from current high levels' would raise federal tax revenues. Moreover, in 1987 after the capital gains tax rate went up, many states including Massachusetts, New York, and California experienced an unexpected drop in revenues. Massachusetts projected a $430 million budget deficit for 1988 of which, according to Robert Tannenwald of the Federal Reserve Bank of Boston, one-fifth to one-third is due to the loss of revenues caused by the higher capital gains tax rate.[1]

Positive effects on economy and distribution of tax burden

Professors James Gwartney and Richard Stroup (1982) have examined the changes in the distribution of the tax burden following the Mellon tax cut of the 1920s and the Kennedy tax cuts of the 1960s. In the case of the Mellon tax cuts, named after Treasury Secretary Andrew Mellon, marginal tax rates that reached 73 per cent in 1921 were reduced to a top rate of 25 per cent by 1926. The effect on the economy

---

[1] 'Capital gains rate wounds Dukakis', *Washington Times*, 13 June 1988. See also 'Dukakis is Facing Critical Test in Massachusetts with $600 million Revenue Gap', *Wall Street Journal*, 16 June 1988.

was positive: 'The economy's performance during the 1921-26 period was quite impressive. Price stability accompanied a rapid growth in real output'.

Gwartney and Stroup found the shift in the tax burden equally impressive. By 1926 personal income tax revenues from returns reporting $10,000 or less dropped to 4·6 per cent of total collections, compared to 22·5 per cent in 1921. In contrast total income tax revenues from returns by people with incomes of $100,000 or more rose to 50·9 per cent in 1926 from 28·1 per cent in 1921. They conclude that

'as a result of the strong response of high-income taxpayers, the tax cuts of the 1920s actually shifted the tax burden to the higher income brackets even though the rate reductions were greatest in this area'.

Their analysis of the Kennedy tax-rate reductions (which cut the top rate from 91 to 70 per cent) yields similar results. In 1965, after the tax-rate reductions, collections from the highest 5 per cent of income earners rose to 38·5 per cent of the total from 35·6 per cent in 1963. In contrast, the proportion of income tax revenues from the bottom 50 per cent of tax returns fell from 10·9 per cent in 1963 to 9·5 per cent in 1965.

In testimony before the Joint Economic Committee of Congress in 1984, Gwartney noted that the Economic Recovery Tax Act of 1981 (ERTA) yielded similar results. The reduction of the top marginal tax rate from 70 to 50 per cent cut the tax rates paid by high-income earners by as much as 28·6 per cent, but tax revenues collected from the rich increased. Revenues from the top 1·36 per cent of taxpayers, the group that most benefited from the rate reductions, rose from $58·0 billion in 1981 to $60·5 billion in 1982. The proportion of the total income tax collected from the top 1·36 per cent of taxpayers rose to 21·8 per cent in 1982 from 20·4 per cent in 1981.

The tax liability of low-income taxpayers fell both in absolute terms and as a percentage of the total. Taxes paid by the bottom 50 per cent of income earners fell from $21·7 billion in 1981 to $19·5 billion in 1982, and the share shrank from 7·6 per cent in 1981 to 7·0 per cent in 1982. Gwartney concludes that:

'far from creating a windfall gain for the rich, as some have charged, ERTA actually shifted the burden of the income tax toward taxpayers in upper brackets, including those who received the largest rate reductions as the result of the 50 per cent rate ceiling'.

This seems to be a general conclusion supported by the empirical evidence from marginal income tax rate reductions in the United States. A Joint Economic Committee staff study, 'The Mellon and Kennedy Tax Cuts: A Review and Analysis' (1982), found that tax cuts in the 1920s and 1960s led to a rise in tax revenue, particularly from the rich. During the decade of the 1920s despite, or because of, the tax cuts, Treasury Secretary Mellon was able to pay off 36 per cent of the national debt.

Effects on Employment and Effort

Massachusetts Institute of Technology economist Jerry Hausman has devoted much time and energy to studying the effect of taxes on work decisions. In a Brookings Institution study, Hausman (1981) reports the following:

'Although income and payroll taxes account for 75 per cent of federal revenues, most economists have concluded that they cause little reduction in the supply of labour and do little harm to economic efficiency. The results of this study contradict that comforting view. Direct taxes on income and earnings significantly reduce labour supply and economic efficiency. Moreover, the replacement of the present tax structure by a rate structure that proportionally taxes income above an exempt amount would eliminate nearly all of the distortion of labour supply and more than half of the economic waste caused by tax-induced distortions'.

In another study Hausman (1983) finds that, using 1975 data, labour supply was 8·2 per cent lower than it would have been without federal income taxes, FICA taxes, and state income taxes. He notes in particular that:

'the effect of the progressiveness of the tax system is to cause high wage individuals to reduce their labour supply more from the no tax situation than do low tax individuals. . . . Of course, this pattern of labour supply has an adverse effect on tax revenues because of the higher tax rates that high income individuals pay tax at'.

Measuring the effects on labour supply of the tax system and of a 10 and 30 per cent reduction in marginal income tax rates, Hausman reports that a person earning a nominal wage of $3·15 an hour worked 4·5 per cent less than he would have in the absence of taxes. He would choose to work 0·4 and 1·3 per cent more after 10 and 30 per cent tax-rate reductions. As income increases, the responses get larger. Taxes cause a person earning $10 an hour to reduce the number of hours worked by 12·8 per cent. A 10 and 30 per cent reduction would induce him to increase his work time by 1·47 and 4·6 per cent, respectively.

Another interesting result of Hausman's work is his calculation of the 'dead-weight loss' incurred by the imposition of the progressive income tax system. He defines dead-weight loss as the amount an individual would need to be given to be as well off after the tax, less the amount of tax revenues raised. Hausman found that there was an average dead-weight loss equivalent to 22·1 per cent of tax revenue collected, which is income that is 'lost' because of taxes. As income increases, so does dead-weight loss. A person earning $10 an hour, according to Hausman, has a dead-weight loss of 39·5 per cent of tax revenue.

Cash transfers reduce work incentive

The impact of income maintenance programmes on the work effect of low-income earners also clearly demonstrates the relative price effects of taxation explained by supply-side economists. The Seattle/Denver Income Maintenance Experiments (SIME/DIME) were the fourth and most comprehensive of the experiments undertaken by the government in the 1960s and 1970s to examine the effects of a cash transfer programme or negative income tax on low-income earners. People were given cash transfers of varying amounts, which guaranteed them incomes whether they worked or not. Their incomes were taxed so that when they began earning income above a certain level, the subsidy was gradually reduced to zero. The purpose of the study was to determine whether a cash transfer would be a more efficient way to transfer income to the poor than the variety of welfare programmes already in existence.

The negative income tax lowers the relative price of leisure and, not surprisingly, the SIME/DIME results, published in May 1983, show 'a significant negative effect on hours worked per year'. Married males participating in the three-year cash transfer programmes worked an average of 7·3 per cent less than they would have in the absence of the negative income tax. Those who participated in the five-year programme reduced their labour supply by 13·6 per cent, demonstrating that work disincentives rise with the permanence of income support programmes. Wives and female heads of households showed a larger response to the cash transfer programme. When the cash transfer experiment ended, the report noted that labour supply increased:

'By the end of the first post-treatment year, labour supply for NIT-eligible husbands had again returned essentially to the same level as that for controls, indicating strongly both that the observed response was indeed a result of the treatment and that husbands can adjust their labour supply fairly rapidly to changed incentives'.

Today in the USA no serious economist any longer denies the relative price effects of taxation (and regulation). The arguments no longer dispute their existence but their precise magnitude. The supply side won, and the Keynesian emphasis that focussed exclusively on the income effects of taxation has been superseded by a broader appreciation of fiscal policy.

IV. IMPLEMENTATION AND RESULTS OF SUPPLY-SIDE ECONOMICS IN THE UNITED STATES

In August 1980, during the US presidential campaign, the view of reputable economic forecasters was that tax revenues in succeeding years would be growing much faster than government expenditures, resulting in rapidly growing budget surpluses within three years. The Congressional Budget Office forecast a surplus of $37 billion in 1983, rising to $96 billion in 1984 and $175 billion in 1985. Reagan's campaign advisers decided to take advantage of these surpluses and hook his presidential candidacy on the emerging supply-side movement in the Congress. These surpluses were calculated allowing for normal growth in government spending and a 40 per cent increase in the defence budget during 1981-85 (Anderson, 1988).

The Republicans promised that, instead of creating new government spending programmes, they would return the money to the taxpayers by cutting tax rates. Despite the tax reductions, both revenues and expenditures would continue to grow absolutely, but the growth of both would be slowed and would decline as a share of GNP, reaching a goal of 19·3 per cent of GNP in 1984 and a balanced budget.

The Reagan Tax Cuts

In August 1981, President Ronald Reagan signed into law an across-the-board 25 per cent cut in personal income tax rates to be phased in over three years with a provision to index the personal income tax in 1985 to prevent inflation from pushing taxpayers into higher tax brackets. In 1986, the President signed a tax reform bill further reducing personal income tax rates with a top statutory rate of 28 per cent (33 per cent for some upper-income ranges), down from 50 per cent in the 1981 bill.

The 1981 bill also substantially reduced the taxation of business income. Tax rates were cut, and accelerated depreciation expanded business saving. In 1982 the administration, panicked by the unexpected recession and large budget deficit, agreed to a tax increase that limited the benefits of accelerated depreciation and the investment tax credit. Despite the 1982 tax increase, depreciation was more rapid and business income was less heavily taxed than it had been before the 1981 tax cut. In 1986 tax rates on business income were further reduced. The investment tax credit was repealed, however, and depreciation periods were lengthened. The overall impact of the 1986 bill has yet to be calculated. The 1986 bill was motivated in part by an effort to reduce the tax distortions that influence the choice of investments. It ignored the more fundamental problem of the tax bias against saving that reduces the overall level of investment due to the multiple taxation of income from saving (Roberts, 1986a). Nevertheless, in the 1980s business saving is up sharply as a share of GNP.

Despite predictions of rampant inflation, the Reagan economy was more successful than anyone thought possible. The Reagan expansion has not experienced the worsening 'Phillips curve' trade-off between employment growth and inflation that led to President Carter's infamous declaration of 'malaise'. Despite the longest peacetime expansion on record and 17 million new jobs, there has been no rise in the rate of inflation. In the 58-month period from March 1975 through January 1980 (the beginning and end of the expansion from the 1974 recession), the unemployment rate fell by 27 per cent, the consumer price index (CPI) rose by 48 per cent, and gross private domestic investment rose by 50 per cent (in 1982 dollars). In contrast, during the first 58-month period of the Reagan expansion (from November 1982 through September 1987), the unemployment rate fell by 45 per cent (about twice as much), the CPI rose by 17 per cent (only one-third as much), and gross private domestic investment grew by 77 per cent (about 50 per cent more).

The Reagan economy is remarkable in many other ways. It has produced the highest manufacturing productivity growth in the post-war period, averaging 4·6 per cent annually since the recovery began in 1982, compared with 2·3 per cent in the 1970s, 2·7 per cent in the 1960s, and 2 per cent in the 1950s. Since the Reagan recovery began, per capita real disposable personal income has grown by 2·6 per cent annually, compared with 1·8 per cent in the 1970s, 3 per cent in the 1960s, and 1·5 per cent in the 1950s.

Moreover, the evidence shows that the tax burden has shifted upward in the Reagan years. The latest Treasury Department data show that, between 1981 and 1986, the share of federal income taxes paid by the richest 1 per cent rose from 18·1 to 26·1 per cent—a 44 per cent increase—while the share of taxes paid by the bottom 50 per cent fell from 7·5 to 6·4 per cent.

The Twin Deficits

Despite these successes, supply-side economics has been given a bad name as a result of the budget and trade deficits. Its critics have blamed the deficits and the 'crisis of the day' (the strong dollar, the weak dollar, the October 1987 stock market crash, the trade deficit, debtor-nation status) on the 1981 tax-rate reduction. Inevitably, they advocate an increase in taxes as a panacea.

The administration's embarrassment over the deficit was compounded by its delay in explaining the deficit. This failure resulted from an act of political opportunism and allowed the President's critics to control the explanation of his policy for almost three-quarters of a decade.

Role of monetary policy

An objective account of the 'twin deficits' must include the role of monetary policy. In early 1981 the Reagan administration asked the Federal Reserve (the Fed) gradually to reduce the rate of growth of the money supply by 50 per cent over a period of four to six years. Instead, while warning of future inflation from the tax cuts, the Fed collapsed the growth of the money supply and delivered 75 per cent of this reduction in 1981. By 1982 inflation was at the low rate the administration had predicted for 1986. The result was the most severe recession in the post-war era and a totally unexpected collapse in the growth of nominal GNP. During 1981-86 nominal GNP was $2·5 trillion less than forecast (Roberts, 1987). The loss of revenues from this collapse of the tax base had not been anticipated, and the result was large budget deficits. Only in February 1988 did the *Budget of the US Government for Fiscal Year 1989* finally acknowledge that the large budget deficits that have plagued Reagan had originated in the '1981-82 economic downturn and the concomitant decline in the inflation rate'.

In early 1982, however, the administration decided to take credit for the rapid fall in the rate of inflation despite the fact that its economic and budget plans had predicted no such result. This attempt to claim credit prevented the administration from holding the Federal Reserve responsible for wrecking the budget and left the White House with 'triple-digit' deficits hanging around Mr Reagan's neck. The administration never recovered from this public relations fiasco.

In October 1987 the Treasury Department study, 'Accounting for the Deficit', belatedly documented that

> 'the business cycle and compounding high interest rates—not changes in tax structure or programmatic spending—are the major causes of the major 1982-83 jump in the federal deficit'.

The Treasury study breaks the deficit down into its three components: structural, cyclical and net interest, which is net of the taxes the government collects on the interest it pays. The structural deficit, the gap between expenditures and receipts at full employment, is the smallest component. Only during 1984-86 did the federal structural deficit approach the levels it frequently reached during the 1966-76 period. On a general government basis, which includes state and local budgets, the budget has been in structural surplus almost continually since 1977. This empirically refutes the propaganda that the tax cuts caused a structural deficit.

In contrast, the cyclical and net-interest components of the deficit are large. Beginning in 1980, the Federal Reserve's high-interest-rate policy and the large cyclical deficits from the recession greatly increased the net interest component. By 1987 net interest accounted for two-thirds of the federal deficit.

High interest rates and inverted-yield curve

Critics have charged that these high interest rates were caused by the budget deficits. The truth is that high interest rates *preceded* the large deficits. An inverted-yield curve, with short-term rates above long-term rates, characterised the economy in 1979, 1980 and 1981. The inverted-yield curve is an unmistakable sign that high interest rates were caused by stringent monetary policy. The federal-funds rate, an overnight rate set by the Fed, was higher than the interest rate on long-term triple-A corporate bonds from October 1978 to May 1980, from October 1980 to October 1981, and from March 1982 to June 1982. In April 1980 the federal-funds rate exceeded the corporate bond rate by 5·57 percentage points and in December 1980 by 5·69 percentage points. In January

1981, when Mr Reagan was inaugurated as President, the gap peaked at 6·27 percentage points. Overall, interest rates peaked in 1981 with the budget deficit unchanged from its previous year's level. The budget deficit peaked in 1986 at three times the size of the 1981 deficit, with the federal funds rate only one-third as high as it was in 1981.

The President and some of his supporters have attributed the budget deficit and debt build-up to Congress's refusal to abide by its own budget rules. Few have been convinced. Although Congress has set aside the Budget Control Act of 1974 and discarded the budgets submitted by the Reagan administration, congressional overspending does not add up to the amount of the cumulative deficit.

Early in 1982, the White House decided to put the tax cuts at risk in order to protect the Federal Reserve's unexpectedly tough anti-inflation policy. Despite its supply-side tone, the administration could not bring itself to discard the Phillips curve inverse relationship between unemployment and inflation. It was an election year, and there was a fear that Congress would force the Fed to reflate, thus adding to inflationary pressures and confirming opponents' charges of 'inflationary tax cuts'. As an internal Office of Management and Budget document put it, 'the recession must not be blamed on the Fed' (Roberts, 1984). By adopting this tactic, the White House ensured that its fiscal policy would be blamed for the deficit.

This tactic did not serve public policy well. It turned the deficit into a political 'football' and pre-empted rebasing the budget to take into account the lower than expected growth path of nominal GNP. In effect, the budget deficit became a political weapon of value to many participants in the political process. Congressional Democrats, who had been denied credit for the tax cut by Reagan's White House staff, used the deficit as a weapon against Reagan's supply-side policy. So did Keynesian economists, who were bitter about the eclipse of their influence on public policy by upstart supply-siders. So did the Republican Establishment, who resented the take-over of 'their' party by populist Ronald Reagan and Jack Kemp. So did some monetarists, who wanted to consolidate 'their' victory over inflation by shifting the public's perception of its budgetary cost to the supply-side tax cut. In turn, President Reagan and some of his staff used the deficit as a weapon against the spending proclivities of the Congress, which systematically buys votes with taxpayer dollars.

Various politicians, elected and appointed, used the deficit greatly to enhance their public visibility. Regardless of which side of the argument a person was on, deficit-mania became a ticket to fame. The deficit was far too valuable politically for either side to have much interest in eliminating it. Moreover, once rival wielders of the deficit weapon realised that the predicted dire consequences of the deficit did not materialise, there was no incentive for any party to accept responsibility for the deficit and to give up its political value and the gains it protected.

The budget process in USA and UK

It is important for British readers to understand the vast difference between the budget process in the UK and the USA. In the USA the Treasury Secretary has no power over the government's budget. Within the executive branch of government, authority over the budget resides in the White House's Office of Management and Budget (OMB). This office, supposedly, has authority over the various federal agencies and departments and co-ordinates the separate budget submissions into a budget for the US Government, which is submitted to Congress.

Congress can do what it likes with this budget, and usually does. When Congress's priorities prove unacceptable to the executive branch, the President's only real power is that of the veto, which can be over-ridden by a two-thirds vote. During most of Reagan's presidency, Congress prevented him from using his veto by combining formerly separate appropriations into a single massive bill that was delivered to the White House only hours before the US Government was scheduled to shut down from lack of funding and/or the Treasury was faced with default on its bonds (Roberts, 1988). The only prospect Reagan had of immediately reducing the deficit was to give up his one real achievement—the marginal tax-rate reductions. Neither Reagan nor his Treasury Department believed that the net budgetary gain from higher taxes would offset the adverse effects on the economy. Neither did the US Congress, which made no effort whatsoever to roll back the Reagan tax cut. Had they wanted to, the Democrats could have easily repealed the 1981 tax legislation over the President's veto.

1981 Tax Cut not to Blame for Budget Deficit

Whatever the merits of shielding the Fed from responsibility for the deficit, it gave rise to blaming the deficit on the tax cut, an erroneous argument with three formulations:

1. **Claim:** The administration made a 'Laffer curve' forecast that the tax cuts would pay for themselves.

   Fact: On 18 February 1981, the administration presented its policy proposals in an official publication entitled *America's New Beginning: A Program for Economic Recovery*. It included a table showing the Treasury's forecast that its tax-cut proposals would lose $718·2 billion in tax revenues over the 1981-86 period. *The budget was based on a traditional static revenue estimate that the tax cuts would lose revenues dollar for dollar. The loss of revenue from the tax cuts was fully anticipated in the budget.*

   It requires neither academic research nor investigative journalism to discover this fact in official government documents. Yet, Martin Anderson (1988) documents that respected academic economists such as Martin S. Feldstein, Walter S. Salant, Alan S. Blinder, William H. Branson, Robert M. Solow, and Herbert Stein were among the many who spread the erroneous accusation that the Reagan administration made a 'Laffer curve' forecast.

2. **Claim:** The administration made a 'rosy' forecast that assumed tax cuts would provide unrealistic economic growth.

   Fact: The administration forecast lower rates of economic growth than the economy had attained during the 1976-80 period of 'stagflation'. Moreover, the Reagan administration's forecasts of economic growth were substantially lower than those of both previous presidential administrations and not sufficiently better than President Carter's final forecast in January 1981 to show much stimulative impact from the tax cut. The Reagan forecast was originally labelled 'rosy' because it combined economic growth with falling inflation—an impossible combination according to the Phillips-curve theorising of the time. It is precisely this 'rosy' aspect of the forecast that proved true. The forecast failed to predict the deficit not because it was optimistic, but because it was *pessimistic* about inflation.

   The administration was influenced by the concept of 'core inflation'. This maintained that inflation was deeply ingrained and could only gradually recede. Consequently, when the Federal Reserve reduced inflation below the administration's forecast, the budget plan collapsed. The spending 'cuts' that were achieved in 1981 were turned into increases in real outlays, and revenues projected on a 'core-inflation' basis failed to materialise. (The Treasury objected to the core-inflation forecast but could not overcome the coalition of Phillips-curve analysts in the Office of Management and Budget and the Council of Economic Advisers.)

3. **Claim:** The administration cut taxes deliberately to create large deficits, which it hid from view with a rigged forecast, in order to create political pressure against government spending. Senator Daniel Patrick Moynihan (Democrat, New York), former budget director David Stockman, Nobel Laureate F. A. Hayek, and a number of academics and journalists have helped to spread this view of a duplicitous Reagan team.[2] MIT Professor Olivier Blanchard's claim (1987) that President Reagan lost his political bet that 'cuts in taxes would create, via deficits, the political pressure to reduce government spending' is an example of the uninformed, careless speculation that characterises academic analysis of Reaganomics. Moreover, it is one-sided speculation. One could just as well say that Congress lost its bet that deficits would lead to higher taxes and a political defeat for Ronald Reagan.

   Fact: The notion that the professional staffs of the Treasury, the Council of Economic Advisers, and the OMB, along with the political appointees, could be organised in a conspiracy to rig a phoney forecast in the most leak-prone administration in history is so far-fetched that it is inexplicable that US Senators, Nobel laureates, and MIT professors can profess to believe it. Moreover, it is demonstrably false. The original deficit forecast failed because it overestimated inflation and the nominal growth path of GNP. If the 'core inflation' theory had proved to be true, or if the Federal Reserve had brought inflation down more slowly in keeping with the forecast, the large deficits would not have materialised.

To see why this is so without having to work through the arithmetic of the budget, assume that the administration made a Laffer-curve forecast and greatly overestimated the revenue reflows from the tax cut. In this event, one would expect revenue collections as a percentage of GNP to fall dramatically below projections. This did not happen.

---

[2] See, for example, Tom Wicker, 'A Deliberate Deficit', *New York Times*, 19 July 1985, p. A27.

The Reagan deficits are associated with a sharp increase in government spending as a percentage of GNP. Tax cuts can cause revenues to fall, but they cannot cause federal spending to rise as a share of GNP. Only programmatic spending increases and cyclical factors can cause the government's budget to grow faster than the economy.

Disinflation and the Deficit

The farm crisis

The Reagan administration's reluctance to criticise the Federal Reserve resulted from a genuine sense of relief that inflation had collapsed. Yet this collapse had enormous economic, political, budgetary and social costs that are still being felt. The farm crisis is one example of the enormous costs of *unanticipated* disinflation. Lower crop prices, high mortgage rates, and lower inflation led to a 46 per cent decline in farmland values since 1979.[3]

The unexpected pace of disinflation helped to enlarge the deficit in more ways than one. Direct government payments to farmers soared from $1·3 billion in 1980 to $17 billion in 1987. During Reagan's first term, farm income and price supports were the most rapidly growing component of the federal budget. The social costs of the farm crisis were also devastating. In Nebraska, for example, the percentage of farmers suffering psychological disorders increased from 10 per cent in 1981 to 22 per cent in 1986, causing some who lost their land to murder their innocent bankers.[4]

The ripple effects of unexpected disinflation in the farm, real estate, and energy sectors are still threatening the stability of the Federal Deposit Insurance Corporation and the Federal Savings and Loan Insurance Corporation. Current estimates are that a federal budget expenditure of $100 billion is required to make good the federal guarantees of the Federal Savings and Loan Insurance Corporation alone. In the face of these almost daily revelations of the budgetary consequences of unanticipated disinflation, it is extraordinary that people still ask why Reagan did not offset the deficit. The very question

---

[3] In 1979 the average value of farmland and buildings per acre was $1,053 (in 1988 dollars) compared to $564 in 1988.

[4] See, for example, 'In Iowa, Mental Anguish Still Racks Families, Taxes Social Workers, Even as Farm Crisis Abates', *Wall Street Journal*, 18 May 1988, p. 70, and Roberts (1986b).

reflects an insouciance to facts and process that is unimaginable to an informed person.

On the international scene, the 1981 tax reduction, even after subsequent tax increases, improved the climate for investing in the United States. Additional credit was needed to facilitate new investment. The Federal Reserve refused to accommodate the increased demand for dollars and allowed the dollar to appreciate sharply. That action, in turn, produced the trade deficit. Moreover, the stringent monetary policy curtailed US bank lending abroad by making it clear that the forecasts of rising commodity prices, such as oil and copper, which had been the basis for the loans, would not materialise. Without an infusion of new funds, debtor countries have been unable to service their debts, adding more strains to the world financial system.

The Capital Account

Critics of the Reagan economic programme point to the twin deficits and to a decline in the personal savings rate as evidence that the tax-rate reductions, far from being a supply-side policy, launched a Keynesian consumption boom that has left America awash with debt at the expense of future living standards.

One strand of the argument is that America is dependent on foreign capital to finance the budget deficit. Table 1 permits a different explanation: instead of exporting our capital, we are financing our own deficit, while foreign capital inflows finance the investments that foreigners want in the USA.

Between 1982 and 1983, when the net identified capital inflow shifted from negative to positive, foreign capital inflows into the USA actually fell by $9 billion. The change in the capital account resulted from a $71 billion fall in US capital outflows. And over the years 1982-84—the period when the story of massive foreign money pouring into the USA from abroad was firmly fixed in the world's consciousness—there was no significant change in inflows of foreign capital into the USA, but capital outflows collapsed from $121 billion to $24 billion, a decline of 80 per cent. This collapse in US capital outflows is clearly the origin of the large trade deficit, which by definition is a mirror image of the capital surplus. Only in 1986—the year of the falling dollar and low US interest rates—was there a dramatic jump in foreign capital inflows. The falling dollar and interest rates may have worried foreign investors in US financial assets, but real investment in the USA was very attractive to foreigners.

TABLE 1

US CAPITAL ACCOUNT, 1980-87

(*$ billions*)

	1980	1981	1982	1983	1984	1985	1986	1987
1. Capital inflow to USA	58	83	94	85	102	130	213	203
2. *Less*: Capital outflow from USA	86	111	121	50	22	31	96	64
3. *Equals*: Net identified capital inflow	-28	-28	-27	35	80	99	117	139
4. *Plus*: Statistical discrepancy and other (inflows)	26	21	36	11	27	18	24	22
5. *Equals*: Net capital inflow to USA	-2	-7	9	46	107	117	141	161
6. Current account balance	2	7	-9	-46	-107	-116	-141	-161

+ implies inflow, – an outflow

Source: US Department of Commerce.

What caused the collapse in US capital outflows? The business tax cut in 1981 and the reductions in personal income tax rates in mid-1982 and mid-1983, together with less attractive investment opportunities in foreign countries, especially in the Third World, raised the after-tax rate of return on real investment in the USA relative to the rest of the world. Therefore, instead of going abroad, the money stayed at home.

US Deficit in Perspective

The memoirs of former Treasury Secretary and White House chief of staff Donald T. Regan (1988) reveal that most of President Reagan's political appointees believed that 'his agenda was unfashionable'. They feared that their support for Reagan's agenda would give them a bad press and damage their future careers. Consequently, they added their voices to those of the President's opponents decrying his economic policy. On 14 January 1983, the anti-Reagan newspaper, the *Washington Post*, asked what the President thinks 'when he reads the latest bulletin (co-authored by his advisers without attribution) announcing that nobody in the country agrees with the President's economic policies'.

In a famous article published in the December 1981 issue of the

Atlantic Monthly, William Greider, a well-known left-wing journalist who was assistant managing editor of the *Washington Post*, revealed that he had established a 'leak' relationship with David Stockman, Reagan's director of the Office of Management and Budget during his first term. Greider's article, 'The Education of David Stockman', appeared at the moment of the Reagan administration's greatest political crisis.[5] An unexpected recession had dramatically altered the deficit outlook, and Stockman was driving Reagan towards calling for a large tax increase in the January 1982 budget. On the heels of the tax-cut victory of the previous August, such a major change in policy would have destroyed Reagan's credibility and made him a one-term President. Nevertheless, Stockman pulled out all the stops and used Wall Street, establishment Republicans and the media in his effort to raise taxes.

Greider's article added to the momentum by damaging the credibility of Reagan's supply-side policy with the public. He drew on his recorded, regular, secret meetings with Stockman and revealed that, early in 1981, the President's own budget director had accused the supply-side policy of being a 'Trojan horse', a trick to cut taxes for the rich. Despite these extraordinarily damaging false accusations, Stockman was not removed from office and used his pulpit for more than three more years to create public myths about the origin and consequence of the 'Reagan deficit'. The fact that a new policy could survive such extreme disloyalty is a testament to the lack of an alternative.

Myth of US 'deficit imbalance'

One of the most influential myths is that the US budget deficit is consuming the investment resources of the globe. European leaders, quick to appreciate any scapegoat offered by Americans, seized on this fantasy as the reason why investment and employment in their own economies was low. This guaranteed that the US 'deficit imbalance' would be a concern of successive economic summits, endowing the 'imbalance' with a long media life. Whereas in fact the OECD's data showed that the US deficit was *less* than the average for the OECD as a percentage of GNP.

The OECD publishes data on 'internationally comparable general government budget balances'. This definition encompasses central,

---

[5] Greider's article later appeared in book form.

TABLE 2

BUDGET DEFICITS

The OECD publishes data on 'internationally comparable general government budget balances'. This definition encompasses central, regional and local government balances, as well as social security financial balances, and is claimed by OECD to represent the 'most widely accepted basis of measurement . . . for international comparisons'. Recent data, along with long-term averages and the latest OECD forecasts, are included below:

General Government Financial Balances	USA	Canada	UK	Germany	Holland	Italy	France	Spain	Japan	Sweden	Australia
				As % of nominal GNP/GDP							
1970-86 (av.)	-1·7	-2·6	-2·8	-2·0	-3·3	-9·4	-1·1	-2·2	-2·1	-0·1	-0·8
1983	-3·8	-6·9	-3·6	-2·5	-6·4	-10·7	-3·2	-4·8	-3·7	-5·0	-4·0
1984	-2·8	-6·6	-3·9	-1·9	-6·2	-11·5	-2·7	-5·5	-2·1	-2·6	-3·2
1985	-3·5	-7·0	-2·9	-1·1	-4·8	-12·3	-2·9	-6·8	-0·8	-3·8	-2·9
1986	-2·4	-5·5	-2·6	-1·2	-5·6	-11·2	-2·9	-5·7	-0·9	-0·3	-2·8
1987 (e)	-2·4	-4·4	-2·1	-1·7	-6·3	-10·3	-2·8	-4·9	-1·2	+3·9	-1·6
1988 (f)	-2·3	-3·3	-1·9	-2·3	-6·3	-10·0	-2·7	-4·9	-1·1	+2·6	-0·3

Others not available

e: estimated
f: forecast

Source: OECD *Economic Outlook*, May 1988.

TABLE 3

FEDERAL DEBT AS SHARE OF GNP

	1973	1986	% change
	per cent	*per cent*	
Austria	10·8	55·9	417·6
Spain	13·8	49·0	255·1
Sweden	22·5	68·8	205·8
Japan	30·9	90·9	194·2
Belgium	54·0	123·2	128·1
W. Germany	18·6	41·1	121·0
Italy	52·7	88·9	68·7
Netherlands	43·2	72·2	67·1
Canada	45·6	68·8	50·9
France	25·4	36·9	45·3
USA	39·9	56·2	40·8
Switzerland	30·3	32·5	7·3
UK	71·8	57·7	–19·6
Weighted Average	*37·5*	*62·1*	*65·6*

Source: Bank for International Settlements.

regional and local government balances, as well as social security financial balances, and is claimed, by OECD, to represent the 'most widely accepted basis of measurement ... for international comparisons'. Recent data, along with long-term averages and the latest OECD forecasts from the May 1988 *Economic Outlook* are included in Table 2. If there has been a uniquely Reagan deficit crisis, it is *not* reflected in this data.

Bank for International Settlements data in Table 3 reveal other interesting comparisons. The USA has one of the lowest ratios of federal debt to GNP in the developed world. Moreover, during 1973-86, a period of the largest deficits in US history, only the UK and Switzerland experienced a lower growth in the ratio of debt to GNP. In the USA the ratio rose by 40·8 per cent, but in Germany and Japan, countries that are often represented as hallmarks of fiscal responsibility, the ratio rose by 121 per cent and 194 per cent respectively.

The unjustified hysteria over the US budget deficit served many purposes, chief of which were to discredit the supply-side policy of restoring people's property rights in their own income and to make a scapegoat of the USA for the failure of European policies to create new jobs. The hysteria produced an unbroken string of erroneous financial forecasts from 1981 onwards. It was alleged that the US budget deficit would cause higher inflation. When inflation collapsed, it was alleged that the deficit would prevent interest rates from falling. When interest rates collapsed, Martin Feldstein, Chairman of Reagan's Council of Economic Advisers, predicted in the 1983 *Economic Report of the President* that the deficit would crowd out private investment and prevent an economic recovery. When the recovery began, it was alleged that the deficits would prevent the dollar from falling and deindustrialise America. When the dollar fell, the 'crisis' was blamed on a budget deficit which, only a few months earlier, was supposed to prevent 'dollar adjustment'. All the while, as important financial publications and renowned economists compiled a record for themselves of being 100 per cent wrong year after year, they maintained that Reaganomics was 'voodoo economics' for predicting that the 1981 tax cuts would pay for themselves—a prediction never made. This extraordinary record of disinformation is devastating for the expectations that academics have for public policy.

US cause of 'global imbalance'?

When inconvenienced by facts, critics still attempt to blame Reagan's policy for causing a 'global imbalance' by making the USA a debtor nation. This view reflects a lack of understanding of supply-side economics and global capital markets; it is an expression of anti-economic thinking that the function of 'rich' nations is to finance 'poor' nations. By becoming a debtor, the USA has ceased to lead the international transfer of resources from rich to poor.

The caricature of the USA as 'the world's largest debtor' is based on faulty accounting that compares older book values of US investments abroad with the more recent values of foreign-owned US assets. When US overseas assets are valued at current prices, the picture changes dramatically. Moreover, during the period of 'concern' over American indebtedness, US income from its foreign assets continued to exceed the income paid to foreigners. But this is not the main point.

The notion that 'mature' industrial countries are natural exporters of capital reflects the old Keynesian stagnation view that they run out of profitable investment opportunities at home. Stagnationists came in for many criticisms, which need not be repeated here, but it is appropriate to add one from a supply-side perspective. The rate of return on investment is an after-tax phenomenon. When tax rates are lowered, the number of profitable investments rises. The imbalance caused by the Reagan administration was to raise the after-tax rate of return in the USA relative to the rest of the world. Instead of moving quickly to catch up, other countries responded with austerity policies that increased and maintained the US advantage. Now that Britain and other countries are reducing their own tax rates, this US advantage will disappear.

The Savings Rate

Critics have also painted a distorted picture of US saving and investment during the 1980s. Analysts have focussed on statistical series that provide the least favourable view, such as growth in the net stock of business fixed capital, net private saving and the personal saving rate, and they have not explained why these statistics are fundamentally misleading. Some analysts have even made international investment comparisons that are not adjusted to take account of the fact that the US national income accounts are unique in classifying public investment as consumption!

Changes in US tax law in the 1980s caused a shift in the composition of investment towards assets with shorter lives that increase business cash flow by generating more depreciation. A comparison on a net basis of US saving and investment behaviour in the 1980s with previous periods or other countries misreads a change in asset mix caused by tax law changes as a decline in investment behaviour. Comparison on a gross basis tells a different story. Despite the recession, during 1980-84 gross business fixed investment averaged 11·4 per cent of GNP, exceeding the 1947-81 average of 10·15 per cent and every five-year average beginning in 1950, including 1960-64, 1965-69, and 1975-79 (Table 4). Moreover, this investment record was achieved despite the volatility in monetary policy and exchange rates and despite the constant hysteria in the financial media.

The growth of real business fixed investment was exceptionally strong during the first two years of the Reagan expansion—a 12·3 per cent annual rate of growth. Investment then slowed during the middle of the expansion until 1987 when there was a renewal of rapid investment. The latest figures suggest that the US economy is entering an unusual second stage of a capital spending boom.

TABLE 4

US BUSINESS FIXED INVESTMENT AS A PERCENTAGE OF GNP

	%
1950-54	9·40
1955-59	9·83
1960-64	9·24
1965-69	10·47
1970-74	10·42
1975-79	10·93
1980-84	11·40
1985-87	10·41
1947-81	10·15
1982-87	10·72

Source: US Department of Commerce.

Reasons for investment slowdown

There are three reasons for the slowdown in investment from the fourth quarter of 1984 to the fourth quarter of 1986:

o Investment in non-residential structures fell at an 8 per cent annual rate as lower tax rates discouraged former tax shelters such as office buildings and other tax law changes shifted investment to shorter-lived assets.

o The sharp drop in inflation and energy prices caused investment in oil and natural gas to decline.

o The long legislative debate over tax reform discouraged investment in general while investors waited to see the final outcome.

Critics point to the decline in one component of the savings rate— the personal savings rate—as proof that the tax-rate reductions did not increase saving. Statistics do show that gross personal saving has fallen as a percentage of GNP. During 1947-81 it averaged 4·8 per cent; during 1982-87 it averaged 3·7 per cent. This decline is not, however, the smoking gun for which critics have been searching. Rather, it is a reflection of demographics and the way saving is measured.

Demographic trends and the savings rate

The coming of age of the decade-long post-war baby boomers has overwhelmed the personal savings rate with a wave of young adults. Young adults have notoriously low savings rates while they acquire homes and furnish them. Furthermore, in computing GNP, rental values are imputed to housing and counted as consumption whether it is owned or rented by the occupant. Any time there is a demographic bulge of young adults forming households, the 'consumption' of housing will rise relative to disposable income as rents are bid up and debt is used to purchase housing and its contents.

Since saving is measured as what is left after consumption, it tends to fall whenever population trends produce a larger proportion of young adults. Edward Yardeni (1988), economist with Prudential-Bache Securities, estimates that demographics account for 68 per cent of the decline in the savings rate during the 1980s. As the demographic trend reverses in the 1990s, the personal savings rate should rise.

Other factors have worked to lower the savings rate in the 1980s. The severe 1981-82 recession brought down both the personal and public savings rates. A tenet of Keynesian economics is that recessions are periods of dissaving. The unemployed cannot save, and savings are drawn down to maintain living standards. The government budget automatically accumulates red ink as tax receipts fall and unemployment payments swell. When a recession's deficits are financed at historically high interest rates, more red ink is produced. Since recessions cause pent-up demand and force consumers to defer purchases, the initial stages of recoveries are also characterised by low savings.

Many economists believe that the extraordinary rise in the values of financial assets such as stocks and bonds also lowered the personal savings rate during the Reagan recovery. They argue that this large increase in wealth caused people to increase consumption, thus lowering the savings rate.

Paradoxically, supply-siders underestimated the rise in wealth that their policy would cause. But no one ever claimed that a tax-rate reduction could fully offset demographic changes or the impact on savings rates of recession and sharp rises in wealth.

The remarkable fact is that the rise in business saving during the 1980s (resulting largely from faster depreciation) has offset the fall in the personal savings rate. Despite the factors working to lower personal savings, the gross private savings rate (which includes personal and business saving) has averaged 16·7 per cent during the Reagan recovery, compared to 16·6 per cent during the 1947-81 period. The supply-side policy has succeeded in maintaining the private savings rate at its post-war average despite the demographic and other pressures operating to push it down.

Some economists have attempted to adjust for some of the factors depressing the private savings rate in order to get a more accurate measure of the impact of the 1981 tax-rate reduction. In a 1986 study, Paul D. Evans and Douglas H. Joines concluded that the incentive effects raised private saving relative to the trend by nearly the same percentage amount 'as that following the Kennedy tax cut'.

The most depressing factor on the US savings rate in the 1980s has been the 1981-82 recession, which pushed the public savings rate deep in the red by swelling the budget deficit. The large cyclical deficit, together with the Federal Reserve's high-interest-rate policy, greatly increased the net interest component of the budget.

Facts confound the critics

The focus on the personal savings rate as a measure of supply-side success allows critics to ignore the adverse impact on saving of demographics, recession, and a rise in wealth. It demonstrates the grinding of axes, not the failure of a policy.

The statistical facts are inconsistent with the picture of the US economy as a consumption-driven machine fuelled by large deficits threatening the world with inflation. Polemicists who claim that the Reagan expansion is nothing but a deficit-fuelled Keynesian consumption binge have to explain what happened to the Phillips curve. Why did the Keynesian policy not work for President Carter? Why did smaller deficits lead to a worsening inflation trade-off for Carter, while larger deficits were accompanied by declining inflation under Reagan? There was a bad recession in 1974-75, but it was not followed by a six-year expansion with low inflation.

If the Reagan tax-rate reductions have brought the American economy to its knees, as so many critics have claimed, why are so many other countries cutting their tax rates? Moreover, even Jesse Jackson, the most left-wing candidate ever to run for the presidential nomination of the Democratic Party, has said that he does not favour a top tax rate higher than 38 per cent, which is far below the 70 per cent rate with which the Reagan era began. Neil Kinnock, leader of the British Labour Party, has said that he no longer favours a rate above 50 per cent, which is far below the punitive rates that the Labour Party used to demand (and impose).

As the old saying goes, 'the proof is in the pudding'. If Reaganomics had brought the US economy to its knees, the USA would be experiencing a massive flight of capital. Instead, since 1982 Americans have curtailed their export of capital, and foreigners have sunk hundreds of billions of dollars into real investments in America. Why should we believe the academic and journalistic critics and not the private investors?

America was a debtor country for its first 300 years. Japan experienced trade deficits for 20 years following World War II. Neither country suffered any damage to its long-run viability.

V. CONCLUSION

In 1956 Swedish socialist Gunnar Myrdal was able to claim of the success of his ideology:

> 'Grand scale national planning is the goal in underdeveloped countries all over the globe and this policy line is unanimously endorsed by governments and experts in the advanced countries'.[6]

No one is making such claims today. In the 1980s, socialist countries everywhere are in retreat from the consequences of their own policies. Privatisation and tax-rate reduction in Britain and France, the collapse of Third World 'development planning', the stagnation of the Soviet economy, and the transformation under way in China have destroyed socialism. The supply-side approach to economic policy is spreading throughout the world, and the revolutionary re-emergence of private property out of communism is an historical watershed. 'It is good to be rich,'[7] declare China's leaders, and these six words are a resounding affirmation of individual incentive.

The effects of disincentives have clearly thwarted the intended results of central planning, government investment programmes, and demand management. On the other hand, there is today an abundance of evidence of the power of incentives. Only free people are productive and forward-looking, but they cease to be free when their property

---

[6] Gunnar Myrdal, *Development and Underdevelopment*, Cairo: National Bank of Egypt Fiftieth Anniversary Commemoration Lectures, 1956.

[7] Cited in Marshall I. Goldman and Merle Goldman, 'Soviet and Chinese Economic Reform', *Foreign Affairs*, Vol. 66, No. 3, p. 570.

rights are sacrificed to interest-group politics and ideologies of government planning.[8]

Reagan brought confidence back—confidence that could even survive year after year of doom and gloom about budget and trade deficits and interest and exchange rate volatility. Confidence returned because of the steps taken to restore private property rights. Tax rates were cut. Regulation was slowed. Inflation fell. Abroad, socialised countries began privatising. The tide finally turned in a 50-year-old war that advocates of economic liberty had been losing. It is extraordinary that even freedom's allies are little inclined to cheer and greatly inclined to blame the expansion of private property rights for the 'twin towers of debt'.

The reconstruction of economic liberty is not complete. The deficit needs to be cut, but in the right way. It is self-defeating to try to reduce the deficit by withdrawing pro-growth incentives. The most successful way of reducing deficits is to encourage the economy to grow relative to the government's budget by controlling public spending and maintaining incentives for economic growth. A high interest-rate policy 'to support the dollar' is at odds with deficit reduction. Instead, private saving needs to be expanded by reducing and eliminating the existing tax bias against saving that results in the multiple taxation of investment income. A consumption-based income tax that excludes saving from the tax base would obviously increase personal saving.[9]

Close attention must be paid to monetary policy. It is just as important to avoid unnecessary restraint on economic growth as it is to avoid inflation. We cannot afford a monetary policy that elects to take only recessionary risks, and we cannot permit the pretence that fiscal policy determines interest rates.

An important function of representatives in diplomatic, economic, and multilateral lending institutions must be to spread understanding of the supply-side policy. Reliance on incentives, markets, and private investments is an easy sell in the light of the unhappy experience of the Third World with development planning, of Europe with socialisation,

---

[8] To see how far we have come, think back a decade to President Carter, battered by worsening Phillips curve trade-offs between inflation and unemployment and without hopeful policy options. Remember the infamous 'malaise' speech signalling the death of hope. Remember the policy-makers' emphasis on incomes policy and industrial policy, which would lead to further erosion of economic liberty. That is where we were, and that is from whence Reagan's supply-side policy has brought us.

[9] See *Blueprints for Basic Tax Reform*, US Department of the Treasury, 17 January 1977.

and of the Soviet Union and China with central planning and economic coercion.

To be deterred from this easy task, and to be thrown on the defensive by a budget deficit, indicates a lack of belief that is inconsistent with leadership. This is especially the case with a deficit that reflects nothing but the failure to rebase the budget to take into account a quicker than expected victory over inflation. A spending freeze for one or two years is all it would take to wipe out the deficit. If, following many years of large increases in federal spending, this small step is considered too drastic, the budget deficit cannot possibly be the dire problem it is claimed, and we should be content to eliminate the deficit more gradually by expanding the economy.

If the spokesmen for economic freedom do not lose their nerve, the extraordinary failure of socialism and central economic planning in the 20th century promises that the 21st century will be one of private property and expanded economic liberty.

This transformation is underway in the USA. After an eight-year struggle with Ronald Reagan, the Democrats have taken steps to reclaim supply-side policy as their own. Michael Dukakis, the Democratic candidate for President in the November 1988 election, rejected the left-wing of his party and chose Senator Lloyd Bentsen of Texas, one of the original supply-side politicians. In 1979 and 1980 the annual reports of the Joint Economic Committee of Congress, under the leadership of Senator Bentsen, rejected a continuation of Keynesian demand management and called for the implementation of a supply-side economic policy. Dukakis himself did not run against Reaganomics or call for a repeal of the supply-side tax-rate reductions.

The campaign against the supply-side policy failed because it was based on false charges, namely that Reagan based his budget on a 'Laffer curve' forecast that the tax cuts would pay for themselves. But no such forecast was made. Moreover, the alleged interest- and exchange-rate effects of alleged 'supply-side' deficits failed to materialise. Furthermore, the US Treasury's important study, *The Effect of Deficits on Prices of Financial Assets: Theory and Evidence*, surveyed the economic literature and found that neither theory nor empirical evidence supports the argument that interest and exchange rates are explained by budget deficits.[10] This conclusion has been reinforced by events since the study's publication.

---

[10] The study, published in March 1984, is available from the Superintendent of Documents, US Government Printing Office, Washington DC 20402.

Faced with a record-breaking successful economy that they can no longer denigrate, some diehard critics have changed their tune. They now attribute Reagan's success to Keynesian deficit-spending and call it their own. It is amusing to watch people simultaneously claim that Reagan's successful economy is based on Keynesian deficits but that supply-side deficits are an enormous threat to the economy.[11] With its critics reduced to such blatant inconsistency and special pleading, the supply side has clearly triumphed.

REFERENCES

Anderson, Martin (1988), *Revolution*, New York: Harcourt Brace Jovanovich.

Blanchard, Olivier Jean (1987), 'Reaganomics', *Economic Policy*, October.

Boskin, Michael J. (1978), 'Taxation, Saving, and the Rate of Interest', *Journal of Political Economy*, 86, April, part 2.

Evans, Paul (1981), 'Kemp-Roth and Saving', *Weekly Letter*, Federal Reserve Bank of San Francisco, 8 May.

Evans, Paul and Douglas H. Joines (1986), 'The Resolution of the Tax Debate', in Victor A. Canto, Charles Kadlec, and Arthur B. Laffer (eds.), *The Financial Analyst's Guide to Fiscal Policy*, New York: Praeger.

Gwartney, James (1984), 'Tax Rates, Taxable Income and the Distributional Effects of the Economic Recovery Tax Act of 1981', Testimony before the Joint Economic Committee, 12 June.

Gwartney, James and Richard Stroup (1982), 'Tax Cuts: Who Shoulders the Burden?', *Economic Review*, Federal Reserve Bank of Atlanta, March.

Hausman, Jerry (1981), 'Labor Supply' in Henry J. Aaron and Joseph A. Pechman (eds.), *How Taxes Affect Economic Behavior*, Washington DC: The Brookings Institution.

---

[11] For examples of this contradictory argument, see Paul Craig Roberts, 'Hoover Democrats', *Wall Street Journal*, 11 August 1988, and 'Yesterday's Economic Doomsayers are Today's Pollyannas', *Business Week*, 15 August 1988.

Hausman, Jerry (1983), 'Taxes and Labor Supply', Working Paper No. 1102, National Bureau of Economic Research, March.

Lindsey, Lawrence B. (1986), 'Capital Gains: Rates, Realizations and Revenues', Working Paper No. 1893, National Bureau of Economic Research, April.

Lindsey, Lawrence B. (1988), 'Tax Reform and Taxpayer Behavior', *NBER Reporter*, National Bureau of Economic Research, Spring.

Myrdal, Gunnar (1956), *Development and Underdevelopment*, National Bank of Egypt Fiftieth Anniversary Commemoration Lectures, Cairo.

Regan, Donald T. (1988), *For the Record: From Wall Street to Washington*, New York: Harcourt Brace Jovanovich.

Roberts, Paul Craig (1984), *The Supply-Side Revolution*, Cambridge, Mass.: Harvard University Press.

Roberts, Paul Craig (1986a), 'The Revolution in U.S. Tax Policy', *National Westminister Bank Quarterly Review*, November.

Roberts, Paul Craig (1986b), 'The Mortals Below: Tragedy on the Farm', *Wall Street Journal*, 6 June.

Roberts, Paul Craig (1987), Testimony before the Senate Banking Committee, 18 February.

Roberts, Paul Craig (1988), 'The Presidency Must Reclaim Its Powers from Congress', *Business Week*, 29 February.

Roberts, Paul Craig, Aldona Robbins, Gary Robbins, and David Brazell (1985), *The Cost of Corporate Capital in the United States and Japan*, Washington, DC: Institute for Political Economy.

Roberts, Paul Craig, Aldona Robbins, Gary Robbins, and David Brazell (1986a), *The House Tax Bill: Does the U.S. Win or Lose?*, Washington, DC: Institute for Political Economy.

Roberts, Paul Craig, Aldona E. Robbins, and Gary A. Robbins (1986b), 'Supply Side Economics and the Cost of Capital', in *Studies in Banking and Finance*, Amsterdam: North-Holland Publishing Company.

Roberts, Paul Craig, Aldona E. Robbins, and Gary A. Robbins (1986c), 'The Relative Impact of Taxation and Interest Rates on the Cost of Capital', in Ralph Landau and Dale Jorgenson (eds.), *Technology and Economic Policy*, Cambridge, Massachusetts: Ballinger.

Sinai, Allen, Andrew Lin and Russel Robins (1983), 'Taxes, Saving, and Investment: Some Empirical Evidence', *National Tax Journal*, Vol. 36, No. 3, September.

US Congress, Joint Economic Committee (1982), 'The Mellon and Kennedy Tax Cuts: A Review and Analysis', a staff study for the Subcommittee on Monetary and Fiscal Policy, 18 June.

US Government, Council of Economic Advisers (1983), *Economic Report of the President: February 1983*, February.

US Government, Department of the Treasury (1987), 'Accounting for the Deficit: An Analysis of Sources of Change in the Federal and Total Government Deficits', by Michael R. Darby, Research Paper No. 8704, 2 October.

US Government, Department of the Treasury (1988), 'The Direct Revenue Effects of Capital Gains Taxation: A Reconsideration of the Time-Series Evidence', by Michael R. Darby, Robert Gillingham and John S. Greenlees, Research Paper No. 8801, 24 May, published in *Treasury Bulletin*, Spring.

US Government, Department of Health and Human Services (1983), *Final Report of the Seattle-Denver Income Maintenance Experiment*, SRI International, May.

US Government, Office of Management and Budget (1988), *Budget of the United States Government for Fiscal Year 1989*, 18 February.

Yardeni, Edward (1988), 'How the Baby Boomers are Changing the Economy', Prudential Bache Securities, Topical Study No. 12, 6 April.

4

REAGANOMICS AND THATCHERISM:
Deficits, Currencies and Monetary Control

Patrick Minford

Professor of Applied Economics,
University of Liverpool

PRESIDENT REAGAN and Mrs Thatcher shared a common rhetoric and set of objectives. Yet their policies diverged in a number of obvious and crucial ways.

'Supply-side economics' got its name from the Reagan team, yet in fact apart from the important tax reform programme there has been little supply-side reform by Reagan; the main item, transport deregulation, was inherited from the Carter administration. In Britain under Mrs Thatcher, after the inflation-fighting campaign of 1979-82, we have had non-stop reform of the supply side—union laws, privatisation, deregulation, local government finance reform, housing, radical tax reform and much else.

One reason is possibly that there was less need for such reform in the already largely private and deregulated US economy. Another reason may be the greater power of Congress, with a Democratic majority in the lower house and lately in the Senate too.

On the budget deficit, the policy contrast is well known. For Mrs Thatcher it was a major plank of counter-inflation policy to get the deficit down. The Reagan policy was until 1985 one of benign neglect; and progress since then has been slow and deliberate. The Gramm-Rudman-Hollings amendment mandating fast progress on pain of automatic cuts in spending has been evaded; the deficit today is still nearly 3 per cent of GDP.

The contrasts are least on monetary policy, where both the Bank of England and the Federal Reserve have eschewed monetary base control in favour of interest-rate fixing in order to stay within longer ranges for money and other indicators. Both here and there, episodes of monetarism have alternated with episodes of 'pragmatic' experimentation with non-money targets like the exchange rate or general economic indicators.

A full comparison is quite beyond the scope of the present paper and my competence. Instead, I want to ask three questions and suggest some lines of discussion.

First, how exactly, if at all, does the deficit matter and did it in these two episodes?

Secondly, was the dollar's volatility the result of pure market exuberance, and therefore a black mark against floating exchange rates; or did it reflect policy shifts rationally sized up in the market?

Thirdly, is monetarism dead or still viable in today's deregulated financial world?

Budget Deficits

There are three main ways of thinking about budget deficits. The most familiar is the 'neo-Keynesian' one (Blinder and Solow, 1973,[1] also adopted for a time by Milton Friedman) in which deficits drive up the rate of interest as government plans stimulate overall spending. However, the extra government bonds held by the private sector add to its wealth steadily as long as the deficit continues and this creates continuous upward pressure on spending and interest rates, which must eventually be brought to a halt by either printing money (which brings interest rates down) or stopping the deficit.

The second way is that of the Minnesota School (associated with Professors Thomas Sargent and Neil Wallace, 1981).[2] The policy implications of this method are similar to the neo-Keynesian. But the route for getting there is different; it is assumed that bonds are issued to one generation when they are young and therefore willing to save.

---

[1] A. Blinder and R. Solow, 'Does fiscal policy matter?', *Journal of Public Economics*, Vol. 2, 1973, pp. 319-337.

[2] T. Sargent and N. Wallace, 'Some unpleasant monetarist arithmetic', *Federal Reserve Bank of Minneapolis Quarterly Review*, Vol. 5, 1981, pp. 1-17.

They cash them in when old and they must then be passed to the next younger generation. Deficits cannot therefore push the stock of bonds beyond some limit set by the savings of the younger generation. Once this limit is reached deficits must stop or else must be financed by printing money, with inflation the result.

The third way is that of the Chicago and Rochester Schools (associated with Professors Robert Barro, 1974,[3] and Robert Lucas—see Lucas and Stokey, 1983[4]). Here it is assumed that households can be treated as immortal dynastic families, fully discounting the future taxes required to pay the interest and principal on government bonds. Because the present value of the tax stream and the bond returns are by definition exactly equal for such immortal households, bonds are not treated as wealth; households are indifferent between holding more or less bonds (and future taxes) in their balance sheets. Hence deficits resulting from lower taxes 'do not matter' provided they are financed by borrowing in the sense that as they occur the private sector is happy to save its extra disposable income against the future taxes it will have to pay.

However, though the Chicago analysis has been used in justification by the Reagan administration, it does not stop there. Since taxes cause market distortions (the 'wedge' between the price paid by the consumer and that received by the producer), we can use the theory of public finance to argue that tax rates should be equal over time; this follows from the same principle that suggests tax rates should be equal across different goods with the same elasticity of demand. Because the size of the distortion rises with the square of the wedge, the total distortion is minimised when the wedges are equalised ('tax-smoothing')—over time and space.

A Flexible Freeze?

Unless the Reagan administration can point to large future net revenue windfalls it cannot really justify its persistent deficit; for it must imply either future tax-rate rises or recourse to inflationary money-printing. Cutting tax rates now, only to raise them later, is sub-optimal, and pointless when the economy is fully employed as now. Hence the

---

[3] R. Barro, 'Are government bonds net wealth?', *Journal of Political Economy*, Vol. 82, 1974, pp. 1,095-1,117.

[4] R. Lucas and N. Stokey, 'Optimal fiscal and monetary policy in an economy without capital', *Journal of Monetary Economics*, Vol. 12, 1983, pp. 55-93.

current debate over the feasibility of a flexible freeze becomes crucial to a judgement on the continued Reagan-Bush deficit, if one takes the Chicago view.

On the other two views, judgement is much easier. It is of course that the deficits have been buying time at the price of making future policy either intolerably deflationary, as surpluses are forced, or highly inflationary as money is printed. Introduce the political constraints and you can probably rule out future surpluses, leaving only future inflation (or 'monetisation').

My own views are that for the sort of prolonged deficit and debt run-up faced by the USA the latter assessment is closest to the truth. Bush will have to act rapidly on his flexible freeze, if the markets are not to lose patience and force US monetary policy into sharply higher interest rates to hold the dollar. But in any case, even on the more sanguine Chicago view, there will have to be deficit cuts if the tax cuts are to stick.

The British situation is now one of massive surplus, even discounting privatisation revenue. In this case, it is much more plausible to argue that the Chicago view holds; debt is falling so rapidly that there are no obvious constraints on debt policy. The question is one of how quickly tax cuts should occur. Tax-smoothing suggests that it is wrong to defer tax-rate cuts.

Earlier, say in 1979, the UK problem was very much the current US one of establishing the credibility of monetary policy when deficits were so large that future monetisation was severely threatened.

Ironically, the wheel of debt and deficits has come full circle; the US has exchanged positions with the UK between 1979 and 1988. Our experience suggests that being a large debtor is not a desirable position to be in. It comes to dominate every issue after a time; only now have we begun to experience the release of being able to ignore the PSBR and look at public issues on their micro-economic merits.

Measuring the Deficit

I have side-stepped measurement of the deficit. In particular, there is the question of adjustment for inflation. If one assumes that inflation will continue for ever at 5 per cent, then it is right to deduct from the quoted deficit figures the inflationary component of debt interest; this is roughly equal to the deficit, which in 'real' terms is thus zero. The trouble with this procedure (the argument is an old chestnut in the UK) is that inflation is supposed to be reduced according to US and Fed objectives. At zero inflation, suppose it to arrive soon or in the early 1990s, the picture is not so rosy, because most of the debt interest is committed for years in advance in money terms; so zero inflation means that its burden in real terms is as great as it seems without adjustment, or in other words with zero inflation there is no inflation adjustment! So if we take zero inflation as a serious target one cannot apply an inflation adjustment to the deficit. Three per cent it is and must be dealt with.

I have deliberately discounted one argument for running deficits— that of browbeating the Congress into agreeing to cuts in public expenditure. I cannot see why Congress should not lock itself into a game of 'Chicken', in which it holds out for tax rises instead. Indeed something like that appears to have happened. Whether one is in a better position to get Congress to agree expenditure cuts with or without the game of chicken, is a question I cannot answer, knowing too little about the political economy of the USA. All I would urge is that the risks of the strategy discussed above be carefully weighed.

The Dollar

It has become a cliché among promoters of international policy co-ordination that the dollar's fluctuations since 1979 demonstrate the inherent instability of exchange markets; thus, they argue for fixed against floating rates and for currency and other intervention when rates cannot be totally fixed.

The theory often advanced for why exchange markets could be naturally volatile centres around expectations. These may be extrapolative, driven by a sort of herd instinct—as the market goes up, people jump on the bandwagon and as it goes down they jump off again.

The theory of 'bubbles'

On one variant of this view people are not mistaken to do this because provided everyone is doing it, it is right to expect it to happen and therefore right to get in on the act. This is the theory of 'bubbles'.

The problem with these theories is that when such bubbles burst or extrapolative runs are reversed, those left holding the market make enormous losses. Smart operators will therefore get out before the end. But then you have a possible *reductio ad absurdum*, if you allow the possibility that everyone is or becomes smart; because then everyone will be getting out before the end, and the end must then come at once. What is needed to make such bubbles happen at all in a market of smart agents is that there be some chance, however small, that the bubble will go on for ever; then some people will hang on until the bubble actually bursts. The trouble with this thesis is that it is hard to make sense of a bubble going on for ever, let alone to posit it as a possibility.

To rebut such an interpretation of currency behaviour on the empirical plane one must offer an alternative interpretation. I do not think this is too difficult for the dollar since 1979.

Modern models of the exchange rate assume that the market looks ahead to all potential developments in fiscal and monetary policy, as well as in the real economy. For example, suppose that a country's money supply is expected to grow 1 per cent a year faster for the next 10 years. Then there will be an immediate and large effect on the current exchange rate. Exactly how large depends on the model; but it could easily be a 15 per cent depreciation at once, with the rate coming back to a long-run fall of 10 per cent—so-called overshooting.

The theory stresses monetary policy most but fiscal policy is also relevant for reasons discussed in the first part of this paper; it raises issues of future monetary policy as limits on borrowing are reached. In neo-Keynesian theory it will also affect real interest rates and so the strength of the currency.

Finally, shifts in productivity affect the real exchange rate. If manufacturing productivity surges in country X, then traded prices which have to compete internationally will fall relative to home prices generally; so if the real exchange rate is measured by relative prices in two countries in a common currency, this will raise the real exchange rate of country X. If an ongoing surge is anticipated, it will lead to an even larger reaction today.

Fiscal and monetary policy swings

So an alternative account of the dollar's swings would look to swings in fiscal and monetary policy, and perhaps too in the supply-side situation. Without going into a lot of detail, it seems clear that up to 1985 there was a general perception that tight money would be used to hold the dollar up and that deficits would be sustained on a steady level, financed by borrowing. While there was concern about future possible monetisation, this was suppressed while money was kept clearly tight and the US Treasury seemed committed to this policy. Devaluation was out as potentially inflationary.

From 1985 all changed. There was a new Treasury Secretary, Mr Baker, concerned about the threat of protectionism (to the political chances of the Republicans as well as the economy), determined to devalue and to reduce the deficit, and putting pressure on the Federal Reserve to go along with looser money. Suddenly the name of the game changed to how much might the dollar be talked down or wrestled down. Markets naturally went into a dive.

The story therefore seems easily told in terms of a very sharp change in US policy—much like that administered by another Texan Treasury Secretary 15 years earlier, Mr John Connally. It would have been surprising indeed if forward-looking markets had not swung on such a change. Models differ on how large the swing should have been; but models always will. The point is that the qualitative account is clearly there, and there is no need to embrace the anti-market and poorly structured theory of bubbles.

Money in a Deregulated World

Under competitive banking, the interest rate on checking deposits tends to equality with the general rate on savings. Hence they cease to be money in the sense that demand for them is determined by their usefulness in transactions. Instead, demand for them is essentially indeterminate because they compete with a host of savings media whose return is the same when adjusted for risk premia.

It is the supply side of the intermediary market that determines the growth of different media; if costs fall in one part, for example banks, then that part will expand, others contract. Also, the total size of the financial sector's liabilities is determined by the efficiency of intermediation; if the sector provides a good service in diversification at low cost, then private savings will be channelled through it rather than directly into shares or loans to primary investors. The more specialised services are on offer from intermediaries, the larger gross liabilities can become as one intermediary redeposits with another.

Such a world of deregulated intermediation, but with currency still necessary for small transactions and issued by a monopoly central bank, is described in Fama (1980 and 1983);[5] I drew on this in characterising recent UK monetary policy (1988)[6] and argued that

---

[5] Eugene F. Fama, 'Banking in the theory of finance', *Journal of Monetary Economics*, Vol. 6, 1980, pp. 39-57; and Fama, 'Financial intermediation and price level control', *Journal of Monetary Economics*, Vol. 12, 1983, pp. 7-28.

[6] P. Minford, 'A monetarist's agenda', *IEA Inquiry*, London: Institute of Economic Affairs, October 1988.

attention should be directed to the monetary base and no longer to wider money aggregates, including M1. The same points appear to apply to the USA where deregulation has clearly sent M1 haywire (see Figures 3-5 at the end of my paper, pp. 73-74). The fact that M2 has not misbehaved in quite the same way is interesting and perhaps points to the role of state-wide banking in residually controlling credit market competition. In the UK deregulation has gone much further with the freeing of building societies from constraints on their portfolio and liability composition; also take-overs of banks may increasingly allow foreign players into the UK High Street.

Monetary Policy and the Banking Revolution

Monetary policy in both countries has had to cope with this banking revolution, which has badly upset the early monetarist targeting machinery. In the UK, the preferred £M3 measure broke up early on; in the USA, M1 lasted for much longer but it too broke up around 1985. Both central banks have accordingly turned to other targets, interspersed with bouts of frank pragmatism.

The exchange rate has popped in and out of the target list. In the UK it retains a shadowy role; in the US it is occasionally mentioned and since the Louvre agreement appears to have had a systematic role.

Here M0 has become the dominant monetary target. In the USA, M2 appears to have assumed that role; the monetary base is monitored but not targeted by the Fed. If, as seems inevitable, state-wide banking starts to crumble, then M2 will presumably disintegrate too, forcing the Fed towards the base.

Monetarists have not traditionally been friends of monetary deregulation (even having at times suggested 100 per cent cash reserve ratios for banks). So deregulation has occurred as part of the supply-side agenda, with the frustration of monetarist rules an unintended by-product. The logic of this revolution has still not fully worked itself out. Once deregulation reduces money to its residual currency component, the scope for raising an inflation tax is drastically curtailed (the monetary base is a small proportion of GDP in both countries); so the main justification for a government monopoly of currency would disappear. Studies, theoretical and empirical, suggest that competitive currency providers can constitute a stable system (Dowd, 1988);[7] so we

---

[7] K. Dowd, *Private Money—the Path to Monetary Stability*, Hobart Paper 112, London: IEA, 1988.

could perhaps see this part of the system privatised in the long run if currency does not disappear altogether in our increasingly cashless society—terminal cures for the problem of inflation.

Conclusions

Here I have examined fiscal policy and found that the current US strategy seems to take unnecessary risks on two views and involve sub-optimal tax-smoothing on a third. Either way, perhaps now we have an opportunity to return towards fiscal orthodoxy; at 3 per cent or so of GDP (assuming zero inflation in the long term) it does not seem to be a particularly intractable problem.

On the issue of the exchange rate the argument has been advanced that it is not so much bubbles as sharp policy shifts that have been at the root of the dollar's volatility.

Finally, on monetary control there has been a common experience of deregulation which has derailed the early monetary targets in both countries. Policy has veered through stop-gaps towards M0 here and M2 in the USA (but probably only an interim solution). Long-term deregulation may make currency privatisation or even disappearance a final outcome.

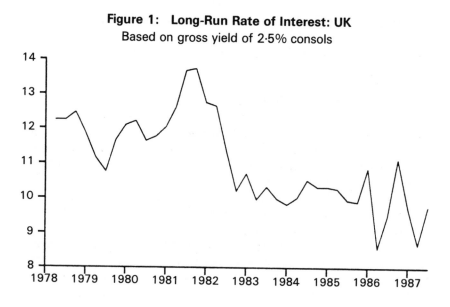

Figure 1: Long-Run Rate of Interest: UK
Based on gross yield of 2·5% consols

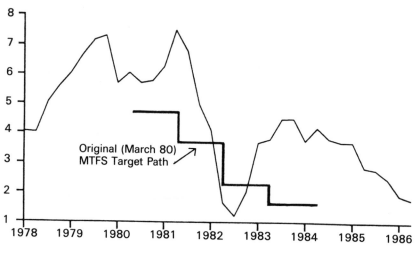

Figure 2: 4-Quarter Moving Average of PSBR/GDP: UK
%

Original (March 80)
MTFS Target Path

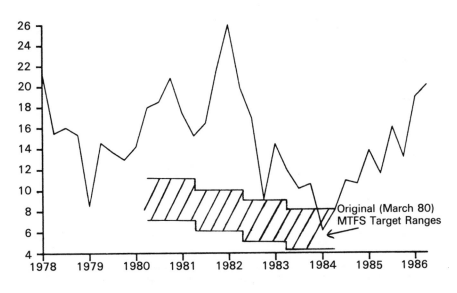

Figure 3: Annual Percentage Growth in Sterling M3: UK

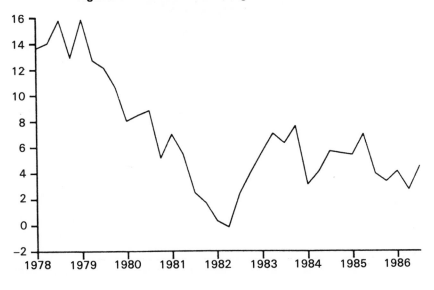

Figure 4: Annual Percentage Growth in M0: UK

Figure 5: US Money Growth

(A) M1 Growth

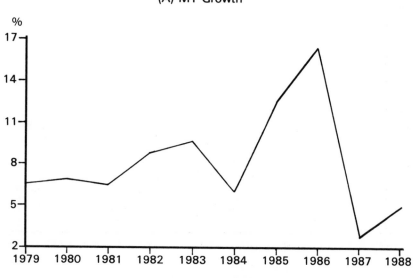

(B) M2 Growth

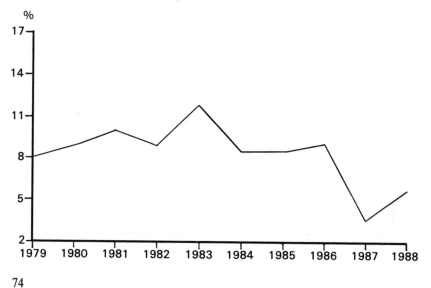

Figure 5: US Money Growth (cont'd)

(C) Currency in Circulation

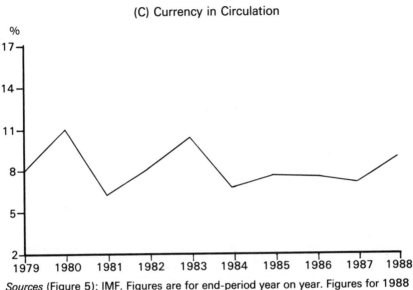

Sources (Figure 5): IMF. Figures are for end-period year on year. Figures for 1988 are the latest month available year on year.

Figure 6: US Dollar Trade-Weighted Index

(1980 = 100)

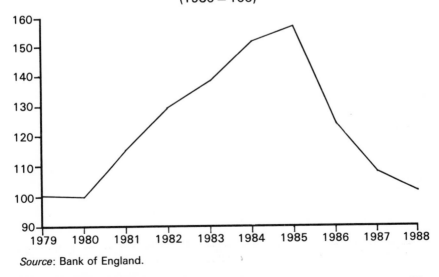

Source: Bank of England.

Figure 7: US: Nominal Long-Run Interest Rate

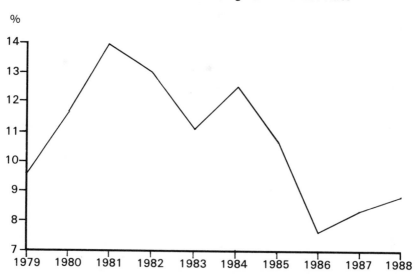

Figure 8: US: Central Government Deficit

(% of GDP)

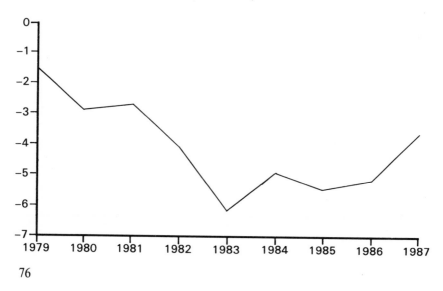

Figure 9: US: Expenditure and Revenue—Central Government

(% of GDP)

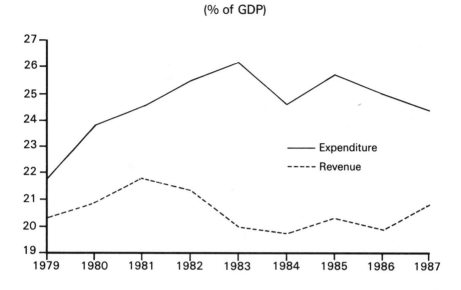

Figure 10: UK: Expenditure and Taxation—General Government

(% of GDP)

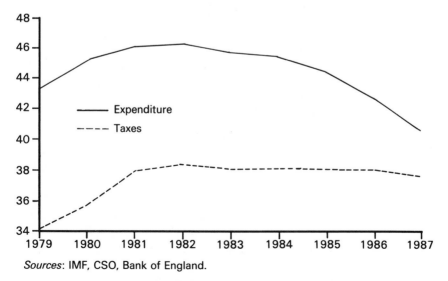

Sources: IMF, CSO, Bank of England.

5

REAGANOMICS, THATCHEROMICS AND THE FUTURE

Irwin Stelzer

Director, Energy and Environmental Policy Center,
Harvard University

ALL ECONOMIC FORECASTING is at best a chancy, and at worst a silly exercise. Indeed, macro-economists can count themselves reasonably successful if the data they gather accurately describe the recent past. And attempts to forecast the future direction of economic policy are even riskier. Not only does one have to have reasonably accurate estimates of future economic conditions; one also has to guess at how politicians will react to those conditions. In the United States, that means guessing at how a Republican President, pledged to avoid tax increases and maintain a strong military, will compromise with a Democratic Congress intent on raising taxes and expanding social programmes. And how an independent Federal Reserve Board will react to that compromise. In Britain, the policy-predicting business is even more difficult: the putative forecaster must read a lady's mind!

So we are peering into a clouded crystal ball when we guess at the futures of the movements that have come to be known as Reaganomics and Thatcherism.

Micro-economic Reforms

President Reagan was elected on a platform pledged to 'get the government off the backs of the people'. This pledge was sufficiently broad, and vague, to mean many things to many people. The business community took it to mean 'regulatory reform'—a reduction in the intrusiveness of government into everyday business decision-making. The hard right religionists had a different understanding: they found nothing inconsistent between Reagan's pledge to reduce the reach of government and their desire to have it and at the same time to regulate social and sexual behaviour. Nor did Reagan. Nor does Mrs Thatcher, who would simultaneously introduce competition into broadcasting and regulate its content.

Such efforts to intrude into the personal lives of its citizens aside (Reagan's, I suspect, can be chalked up to political expediency, Thatcher's to a real conviction that nanny knows best), both Reagan and Thatcher did make considerable progress in shrinking the role of government, and in expanding the reach of market forces in the micro-economy. Both did so, first, by taming the trade union power that had so adversely affected the inflation-employment trade-off. The President successfully broke a strike by air traffic controllers in 1981, at a considerable short-term cost in traveller inconvenience. The Prime Minister equally successfully broke a strike in 1984-85 by coal miners determined to impose their leader's political agenda on an electorate that had rejected it.[1] As with the air traffic controllers' strike in America, the short-term costs were considerable, the long-term benefits even more substantial.

In both countries the principal gain from taming public sector unions was not the direct saving in wage payments to the affected workers. Rather, it was the successful signalling to the US private sector that the government would not be frightened by the prospect of public inconvenience into intervening in labour disputes, and to the UK private sector that a new, non-inflationary attitude towards wage settlements by private sector employers would receive government support. In America, this contributed to a record stability in unit labour costs; in Britain, it provided an atmosphere and a legal climate in which courageous revolutionaries such as Rupert Murdoch[2] and Eric Hammond could sweep away Luddite work rules which, until then, had prevented British industry from taking advantage of modern technology, and imprisoned it in a declining spiral acceptable to the

---

[1] In this she had considerable help from the brilliant advance planning of CEGB chief Walter Marshall, now Lord Goring.

[2] The author is a sometime consultant to Mr Murdoch.

ruling soft left of tenured academics, genteel, BBC-loving intellectuals, and paternalistic, 'wet' Tories.

Regulatory Reform—the Records Diverge

It is in the area of what I shall call regulatory reform that Reaganomics and Thatcherism diverged. In America, the deregulation movement begun under Carter was pursued with considerable vigour and success.[3] Airline deregulation had proved popular: more passengers were moved more cheaply to more places. This policy of substituting competition for regulation was extended to energy, where most prices were decontrolled, to communications, finance, and transport. Perhaps more important, a bias in favour of the proliferation of rules governing business activity was changed to a bias against such proliferation. Bureaucrats were required to justify new rules by demonstrating that their benefits exceeded their costs, and were enjoined to apply existing rules by relying more on incentives and less on commands.

Opposition to deregulation in America

It would be foolish to claim that this regulatory reform movement was *uniformly* successful. Massive opposition by the Congress and liberal jurists combined with political trimming by the administration to preserve some of the counter-productive regulations which unnecessarily inflate costs. And a Chicago-school dominated Antitrust Division failed to do all it should to prevent the spread of business practices that weakened competition in some industries.

But the basic thrust of policy was to replace regulation by competition. In some cases this was accomplished by legislation, such as that repealing energy price regulations. In other cases it was accomplished by appointing pro-competition partisans to chair key

---

[3] 'The verdict of the great majority of economists would, I believe, be that deregulation has been a success—bearing in mind . . . that society's choices are always between or among imperfect systems, but that, wherever it seems likely to be effective, even very imperfect competition is preferable to regulation . . .' (Alfred E. Kahn, *The Economics of Regulation: Principles and Institutions*, Cambridge, Mass.: The MIT Press, 1988, p. xxiii.) Kahn thus seems to join me in disagreeing with William Niskanen's conclusion that 'the failure to achieve a substantial reduction in or reform of federal regulations . . . was the major missed opportunity of the initial Reagan program'. (William A. Niskanen, *Reaganomics: An Insider's Account of the Policies and the People*, New York: Oxford University Press, 1988, Chapter 4.) Despite its subtitle, this is a comprehensive and balanced appraisal of the Reagan policies, not a 'kiss and tell' book of the Don Regan genre.

regulatory agencies: the Federal Energy Regulatory Commission's vigorous new leader, for example, eased entry into power production, opened access to transmission lines, and supported states' efforts to substitute bidding for administrative determination of prices, all pursuant to the same legislation under which her less competition-minded predecessors had operated.[4]

Perhaps even more important was what the Reagan administration did not do. It did *not* attempt to prevent the re-structuring of American industry by so-called 'predators', arrivistes who took over companies, dismissed sleepy managements, and took apart conglomerates, the separate parts of which were worth more than the whole. It did *not* attempt to interfere with the development of new debt instruments, instruments which enabled new entrepreneurs to substitute cheaper debt for more expensive equity; to break the commercial banks' stranglehold on access to credit; and to restore the long-broken link between the ownership and management of American businesses.[5] And it did *not* accept many of the recommendations of panic-stricken commentators on the October 1987 stock market 'crash' that it institute draconian measures to reduce so-called 'excessive volatility'.

It is in this field of micro-management that comparisons between Reaganomics and Thatcherism are most difficult. Both leaders believed in privatisation, but for Mrs Thatcher, who inherited an economy dominated by state-owned enterprises, this was clearly a higher priority than it was in America, where state ownership is less pervasive. Thatcherism's success in converting state-owned to privately-owned enterprises needs no elaboration here: it is a programme so radical in conception, and so successful in operation, as to have won the highest form of flattery from other nations—imitation.

---

[4] Regulation is a field in which men and women matter. Just as Carter appointee Alfred Kahn had used his chairmanship of the Civil Aeronautics Board to free entry into the airline business, so Reagan appointees Norman Fowler and Martha Hesse used their chairmanships of the Federal Communications Commission and the Federal Energy Regulatory Commission, respectively, to introduce competition into the communications industries (Fowler) and electric and gas industries (Hesse). For a good discussion of the 'men do matter' thesis, see Thomas K. McCraw, *The Prophets of Regulation*, Cambridge, Mass.: Harvard University Press, 1984.

[5] Irwin Stelzer, 'The Selling of America' and 'The S.E.C. vs. Drexel Burnham Milken', *American Spectator*, June 1988 and November 1988, respectively.

Lack of emphasis on competition in UK privatisations

It has not, however, been accompanied by any great emphasis on competition. British Telecom was shoved into the private sector with substantial protection against the entry of all save one competitor. British Gas was converted from a state-owned, fully integrated monopoly into a private sector, fully integrated monopoly. A privatised British Airways was permitted to acquire the one company capable of competing with it across-the-board, despite the presence of other willing and able domestic and foreign acquirers. And competition policy, while very much more coherent than it has been in the past, remains riddled with vague 'public interest' criteria and an anti-leveraging bias that makes the market in companies less robust than it might otherwise be.

Most important, regulatory programmes to require those with monopoly power to maintain service and reduce prices to competitive levels have been slow in evolving. This is, I think, due to some confusion about the proper role of regulation. The Government abhors regulation, as it should. But where Adam Smith's invisible hand is atrophied, where competition is unattainable, the long arm of government is a necessary substitute. Competition, where attainable, should be the goal of public policy. But where substantial, unavoidable monopoly power exists, effective regulation of prices, profits and service quality is an unfortunate necessity. This the Thatcher Government persistently refuses to recognise.

None of these failings, however, can detract from the basic success of Thatcherism in converting sluggish, over-manned enterprises, responsive only to politicians, into leaner companies, struggling to understand what consumers want, and dependent on wooing investors' capital, rather than on capital conscripted from taxpayers. Unless we are prepared to let the perfect be the enemy of the good, then both Reaganomics and Thatcherism must be accorded generally good marks in the area of micro-economic reform. Reagan has created a presumption against excessive regulation, Thatcher against state ownership. But what of the future?

What Future for Reaganomics and Thatcherism?

Here it is useful to consider, first, the likely course of events in America. My suspicion is that the vaunted pragmatism of President George Bush and his team means that we have come to the end of the movement towards further micro-economic reform. His desire for better relations with regulation-inclined Democratic congressmen will probably preclude major efforts to roll back government regulation. And President Bush certainly seems more willing than his predecessors to accept environmental regulations demanded by political, rather than economic, considerations. His retention of an establishment figure, one well liked by the teachers' union, as Secretary of Education, suggests that education vouchers and other devices to convert school systems from producer-dominated to consumer-dominated institutions will not be vigorously pursued. His retention of the author of the Brady Commission Report on the stock market 'crash' as Secretary of the Treasury may encourage reconsideration of Brady's unfortunate recommendations for tampering with securities markets. And the appointment of James Baker as Secretary of State, whatever its other advantages, is not likely to reduce government intervention in foreign exchange markets. Reaganomics, at least in its micro-aspects, RIP.

Thatcherism, of course, will not soon be affected by a change in leadership. So we can expect a continuation of efforts to make various social services a bit more responsive to consumer demands, and somewhat more efficient. We can also expect a continuation of the transfer of assets from the public to the private sector. But we should not expect any systematic determination of the role to be accorded to competition. If the regulatory scheme thus far advanced for electricity is any guide, we can also expect a continued inability to cope with situations in which effectively competitive markets are not attainable. And markets will not determine what appears on British television screens, or which mergers shall in fact occur. The former job will be left to establishment censors, the latter to regulators who will continue to review mergers for their 'public interest' implications, rather than solely for their competitive impact.

But all is not lost, for the great triumphs of the Reagan and Thatcher reforms will remain intact, more or less, in the USA and the UK. And they are likely to spread to large portions of the rest of the world, most notably to the USSR. Gorbachev would certainly like to emulate his admirer, the Prime Minister, by privatising at least some sectors of Russia's economy. And he would like to emulate the President by substituting prices for central directives as an allocative tool. So, too, in Latin America, where halting efforts at privatisation and liberalisation are being made, or at least talked about, in an effort to reverse years of economic decline.

In short, the pace of micro-economic reform associated with Reaganomics and Thatcherism may be about to slow in their respective home countries, while it quickens in the rest of the world.

Macro-economic Management

Fortunately, much less need be said about the macro-economic aspects of Reaganomics and Thatcherism. That ground has already been well ploughed, in the case of Reaganomics,[6] and is now in the process of being ploughed, in the case of Thatcherism, as the Chancellor's high-interest-rate approach to controlling inflation attracts close scrutiny.

The tools of macro-economic analysis are far less precise than those available to micro-economists. Indeed, reading through the claims for and the criticisms of Reagan's policies might make one wonder whether anything of value can be said at all. The recent history of macro-economic theory suggests, at the least, that the subject be approached with caution. Keynesians fell into disrepute when their nostrums were seen to produce, first, world-wide inflation, and then stagflation. The monetarists who succeeded them were soon embarrassed by the fact that they could not define 'money', the key variable in all their equations. Then came the 'rational expectations school'. These economists think the world consists of all-wise economic players, operating in omnipotent markets that see all, know all and accurately discount all. They have been tactfully silent since October 1987, when the market changed its rational expectation of stock values by hundreds of billions of dollars in a few hours.

Let me, nevertheless, attempt a few conclusions. First, it seems fair to say that both Reagan and Thatcher should be credited with similar achievements. Both succeeded in wringing virulent inflation out of their economic systems, Reagan with the help of Paul Volker's Federal Reserve Board. And they paid a price—large-scale unemployment. But the willingness of society to bear the pain was demonstrated by the fact that both were re-elected.

Thatcher and Reagan also succeeded, eventually, in establishing patterns of long-term economic growth in their countries, for a record period in the case of America. And both succeeded in enacting tax codes

---

[6] See Niskanen, *op. cit.*, and Benjamin M. Friedman, *Day of Reckoning: The Consequences of American Economic Policy Under Reagan and After*, New York: Random House, 1988.

which are, on the whole, more likely to encourage entrepreneurship than were the codes in place when they were elected.

Both, however, failed to produce the macro-economic utopias used by opposition parties as the yardstick against which to measure the success of incumbents' policies. Reagan has his twin budget and trade deficits, Thatcher her mounting balance-of-payments problems.

The Reagan budget deficit has been laid at the door of the Kemp-Roth tax cuts,[7] and of Reagan's defence build-up. The case for such a position seems to me unproven. The tax cuts did no more than keep federal tax receipts at about the same level, relative to GNP, as they had been during the Carter administration. Revenues from income tax on individuals remain in the 8-9 per cent range characteristic of the post-World War II period. All this *after* the Kemp-Roth tax cuts. And defence spending, while above the level of the Carter years, accounts for about the same percentage of GNP as it did in the Kennedy-Eisenhower peacetime years. The Reagan failure was in not persuading Congress to rein in non-defence expenditures.

But this failure is, in the end, a reflection of the fact that the American people have consistently voted for a Republican president pledged to cut taxes and increase defence expenditures, and a Democratic congress pledged to maintain, indeed expand, social programmes. The budget deficit, then, is a result, in part at least, of America's unwillingness to choose. It is also a result of the budget process, which permits congressmen to trade with one another to gather support for pet spending programmes, while denying the one office-holder with responsibility for the totality of those decisions the ability to say 'yes' to some, and 'no' to others.

Trade deficit—too little saving

The trade deficit is another matter. It is fashionable to blame America's trade deficit on the budget deficit. But how then to explain Britain's trade deficit, which exists side-by-side with a healthy budget *surplus*? Or the fact that Japan's huge budget deficits co-exist quite comfortably with large trade surpluses?[8] The answer, of course, lies in

---

[7] See Friedman, *ibid.*

[8] 'Importantly, the alleged positive correlations between deficits on the one hand and interest rates and exchange rates on the other have not been supported by empirical analysis.' (Mickey D. Levy, 'Origins and Effects of the Deficit', in David Boaz (ed.), *Assessing The Reagan Years*, Washington DC: The Cato Institute, 1988, p. 46.)

the savings rates, too low in the USA and the UK, too high in Japan. If Reagan and Thatcher erred, it was in not increasing the incentive to save, while reducing incentives to spend, incentives such as special tax treatment of home mortgage interest and company cars. To be sure, both leaders have begun to chip away at these consumption-inducing privileges, and Reagan attempted to encourage savings with a variety of special programmes. Clearly, more remains to be done.

But in the long run these problems are largely irrelevant to the eventual ability of Reaganomics and Thatcherism to survive. America's deficits will gradually subside, as real defence spending falls, the economy grows, and the dollar drops. And Britain's trade deficit will drop, as high interest rates squeeze consumer purchasing power. What will matter, in the end, is the electorates' perception of the fairness of the Reagan and Thatcher revolutions.

In America, the 'fairness' debate takes two forms. One is an argument over intergenerational equity. We have, according to Reagan's critics, lumbered future generations with a mass of debt—in effect, we have sold our children's birthright for a mess of Toyotas, television sets and weapons systems. But this argument does not withstand close scrutiny.[9]

A good part of the budget deficit, especially early in the Reagan years, stemmed from two sources: the 1981-82 recession, which cut receipts and increased outlays, and the defence build-up. Deficits during the recession were large, but in the end a price worth paying. They bought our children far more than a mess of pottage: they restored stability to the currency; laid the basis for a steady, record economic expansion that has put them to work in unprecedented numbers; and brought down the interest rates that were making it difficult for them to buy cars and homes.

And the budget deficits produced by the defence build-up may well prove to be the best investment we ever forced the next generation to make. By showing the Russians that we were prepared to prevent them from gaining overwhelming military superiority, Reagan forced them to the bargaining table. Whatever one thinks of the deal he eventually struck, no one can deny that it created the possibility of future cuts in defence expenditures, cuts which will ease the burden borne by the future generations about which Reagan's critics profess such concern.

---

[9] The discussion on intergenerational equity is from my review of Friedman's *Day of Reckoning, op. cit.* See *Commentary,* January 1989.

Is income distribution 'fair'?

The second aspect of the 'fairness' debate, in both our countries, relates to income distribution. Briefly stated, critics argue that the rich have become richer, the poor poorer under Reagan and Thatcher. I shall not attempt here to wade through the data necessary to adjudicate that dispute. Rather, I should like to point out that it is essentially irresolvable. Tax cuts for the higher earners clearly directly benefit the more fortunate. But they also increase the total taxes paid by that group, and encourage the risk-taking that creates jobs for others. Deregulation adversely affects the wage levels of workers formerly protected from competition, but increases the welfare of consumers. Airline unions in decline mean cheaper air fares; coal unions in decline mean lower fuel and electricity prices.

In short, like all revolutions, those led by the US President and Britain's Prime Minister created both winners and losers. Unfortunately, the losers know who they are, and who to blame. The winners, after a while, are not so sure they have won, or are inclined to attribute their victories solely to their own efforts. The result is a gradual erosion of support for further change. In America, that desire to preserve gains rather than push on to new frontiers has given us George Bush, as opposed to, say, Jack Kemp, the proponent of further rapid movement down the Reagan path. In Britain, it has created an atmosphere which almost certainly—and perhaps quite properly—will militate against the adoption of further programmes which seem to benefit high earners, and probably mandate increased expenditures on those at the lower end of the income scale.

In sum, Reaganomics has been fun, but Reaganauts will likely be, if they have not already been, converted from a conquering vanguard into a heroic, increasingly petulant rearguard, fighting to hold rather than gain ground. Thatcherism, too, has been fun—at least for the radicals among us. Its time has not yet passed, and may not, if it can continue to deliver higher living standards and a new sense that its benefits are being fairly distributed. And the leaders of and participants in both movements may soon be debating whether Gorbyism is the true heir of their revolutionary achievements.

6

REAGANOMICS –
A UK PERSPECTIVE

Alan Budd

Chief Economic Adviser,
Barclays Bank PLC

REAGANOMICS AND THE REST OF THE WORLD

WE ARE ALL exposed to changes in the US economy. Their recessions and booms affect us all. Under a régime of fixed exchange rates, their inflation becomes our inflation. If they choose to run a large balance-of-payments deficit they will rely on our surplus savings. It is worth considering briefly how Reaganomics affected the rest of the world. I am concerned with actions rather than ideas; thus Reaganomics is particularly associated with conditions in which tight monetary policy was combined with lax fiscal policy. I am less concerned with the supply-side aspects of Reaganomics, although as consumers we should welcome supply-side improvements whenever they occur.

Charts 1 to 7 illustrate the main developments. The rest of the world is represented by Japan, Germany, France, the UK, Italy and Canada. Thus 'the world' consists of the Group of Seven economies.

Chart 1 shows industrial production. There is clearly a close match between the timing and direction of the fluctuations, although the amplitude is rather greater in the case of the United States. A plausible account of these movements would run as follows. 1979 was a reasonably strong year for economic growth. It represented the last

Chart 1: Industrial Production
USA v OECD 'Big 6'

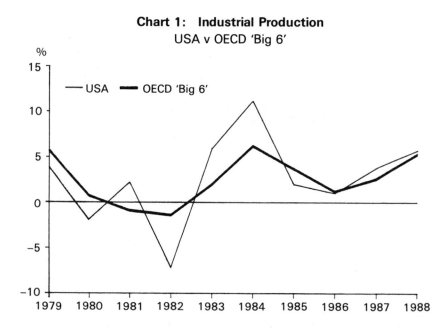

attempt at a co-ordinated expansion of demand, following the Bonn economic summit of 1978. But the boom (and the fall of the Shah) produced the conditions for the doubling of the oil price in 1979 and the recession of 1980-81. The US economy grew slightly in 1981 but by 1982 the tight monetary conditions of the Reagan administration drove the US into recession and the rest of the world followed. After 1982 the relaxation of monetary policy and the rapid expansion of the budget deficit generated a rapid boom in the US economy which was accompanied, albeit in a more subdued form, by the rest of the world. That phase of expansion lasted until 1984 since when economic growth has been maintained steadily at about the pace of the growth of productive potential, with some acceleration in 1988.

The Inflation Cycles

Chart 2 shows inflation, as measured by consumer prices. There is, again, a close matching between the two cycles. Inflation reached a higher peak in 1980 in the USA than in the rest of the world, but from 1982 to 1985 it stayed below the world rate. For the past two years, inflation in the USA has run at slightly above the world rate.

Chart 2: Consumer Prices
USA v OECD 'Big 6'

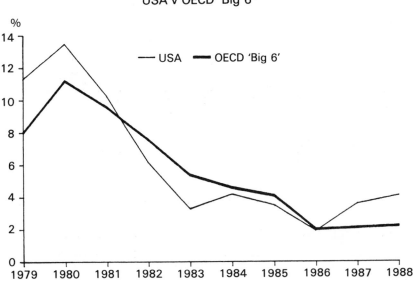

Those conjunctions of movement do not necessarily indicate that actions in the USA affected the rest of the world. There are, however, simple and plausible theories which suggest that short-run changes in demand will be transmitted to the rest of the world through trade flows unless (a) the rest of the world is operating at full capacity, or (b) governments in the rest of the world take steps to offset the trade effects.

During the period from 1981 to 1984 the effect of the US cycle was rather muted compared with previous cycles. There was some tendency for the policy stance in the rest of the world to remain fairly tight during this period. I believe there are two explanations. The first is that the other major members of the OECD accepted the British view that fiscal restraint was an essential accompaniment of monetary restraint. They were therefore tightening fiscal policy as the US was relaxing its fiscal stance (Chart 3). The second is related to Chart 2, which shows that, after 1981, the US was able to bring its rate of inflation down relative to that in the rest of the world. Part of the mechanism by which this happened is shown in Chart 4, which shows the movement in the weighted value of the dollar. It rose strongly, both in nominal and real terms, up to the beginning of 1985. That

Chart 3: Measures of Cyclically Adjusted Deficits
As % Nominal GDP

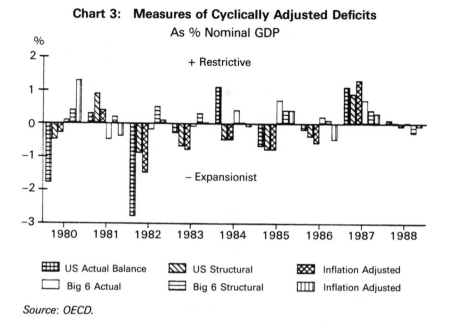

US Actual Balance   US Structural   Inflation Adjusted

Big 6 Actual   Big 6 Structural   Inflation Adjusted

Source: *OECD.*

Chart 4: US Nominal and Real Exchange Rates
Index 1980 = 100

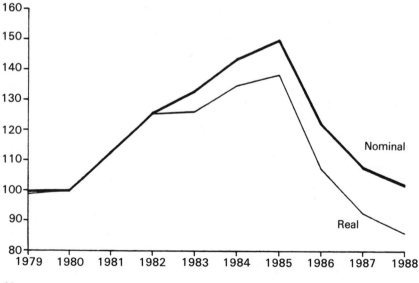

process was extremely helpful in allowing the US to enjoy a rapid expansion of output while inflation fell or was kept low. But the success of the US was achieved at the cost of the rest of the world. The appreciating dollar made it more difficult for the rest of the world to bring its own rate of inflation down and therefore there was a relative tightening of fiscal policy in the rest of the world. That tightening of fiscal policy helped release the additional resources being absorbed by the US as it ran its large balance-of-payments deficit. The real appreciation of the dollar also helped direct production towards meeting US demand.

Patterns of Interest Rates

Another aspect of the story is shown in Charts 5 and 6. Since interest rates are highly endogenous it is dangerous to interpret them directly as responding to deliberate policy actions. One can, however, offer the following explanation for what happened. The background is one of an open world financial system dominated by conditions in the USA. Chart 6 shows the rapid rise in the US real interest rate early in President Reagan's term of office as the counter-inflationary policy took grip. Real interest rates stayed high while the dollar continued to appreciate, and have fallen since 1984. A plausible explanation is provided by a policy shock in which a tightening of monetary policy had the conventional short-term effect of raising the real interest rate. (It has also been suggested that interest rates rose in anticipation of the widening US budget deficit.) Real interest rates stayed high in the US in response to the demand shock of the widening deficit. Because of the scale of the US economy, both the tightening of monetary policy and the subsequent increase in domestic demand caused a worldwide increase in real interest rates. It is also possible that the authorities in the rest of the world kept interest rates high in response to the dollar appreciation.

Finally, given President Reagan's objective of achieving healthy financial markets, Chart 7 shows the movement of share prices. I am not sure how one measures 'health' in this context.

The Effects of Reaganomics

How might one summarise the effects of Reaganomics, as practised, on the rest of the world? President Reagan's policies were directed at the USA. He wanted to cut the rate of inflation and to improve its supply-side performance. Any impact of his policies on the rest of the world

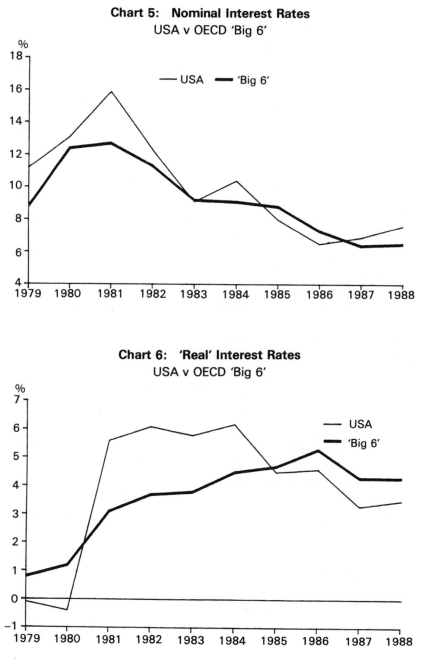

Chart 5: Nominal Interest Rates
USA v OECD 'Big 6'

Chart 6: 'Real' Interest Rates
USA v OECD 'Big 6'

Chart 7: Share Price Indices
USA and UK

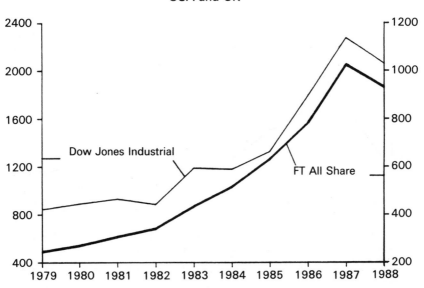

would be incidental although, as William Niskanen has reminded us,[1] one of the key elements of the Programme for Economic Recovery was the aim to restore a stable currency and healthy financial markets.

I have not attempted a rigorous study of the effect of US policy under President Reagan on the rest of the world, but I believe that the following summary is fair:

o the tight US monetary policies of 1981-82 induced a recession in the US, the effects of which were felt throughout the world;

o those monetary policies brought down inflation in the USA and contributed to the fall in inflation outside the USA;

o the fiscal expansion from 1982 onwards helped to generate a rapid recovery in the USA;

o that recovery also raised growth in the rest of the world but the effect was partly offset by the maintenance of more cautious policies outside the USA;

o the policies have been accompanied by a considerable rise and fall in

---

[1] In his paper, 'Reaganomics: A Balanced Assessment', above, pp. 17-22.

the real value of the dollar. Those movements were no doubt disturbing to world trade, although the attempt to stabilise the exchange rate during 1987 almost ended in catastrophe.

A possible lesson from all this is that we would prefer a world which avoided major policy shocks, particularly if those shocks emanate from the USA, though we can sympathise with the President's wish to cut inflation rapidly when he first came to power.

REAGANOMICS AND THATCHERISM

Is Thatcherism the same as Reaganomics? One can ask this question in relation to what was preached and what was practised. I shall suggest that there were close similarities in terms of ideas but that some major elements of Reaganomics have been far more successfully introduced in the UK than in the USA.

William Niskanen has helpfully listed the four 'key elements' of the Programme for Economic Recovery as follows:

o a budget reform plan to cut the rate of growth in federal spending;
o a series of proposals to reduce personal income tax rates by 10 per cent a year over three years and to create jobs by accelerating depreciation for business investment in plant and equipment;
o a far-reaching programme of regulatory relief;
o in co-operation with the Federal Reserve Board, a new commitment to a monetary policy that would restore a stable currency and healthy financial markets.

That programme was presented by President Reagan to Congress in January 1981. The first three elements are concerned with micro-economic policy and the fourth with macro-economic policy. The thinking behind the micro-economic measures can be presented as follows. Mr Reagan believed, as William Niskanen says, that government is more likely to be the source of than the solution to the perceived problems of the time. Thus it was important to reduce the government's direct role in economic activity, through its spending and through its regulatory powers. Those changes would improve the supply potential of the economy. It would also be improved by cuts in personal income tax. A particularly optimistic view was that the supply-side effects would be so strong that cuts in tax rates would actually be associated with a rise in tax revenue. While President Reagan may have believed that that was the case, it does not appear to be a necessary part of Reaganomics.

As Niskanen has pointed out, the original statement of Reaganomics did not include a balanced budget as a specific objective of economic policy. It was, however, assumed that the combined effect of the policy changes would lead to a balanced budget by the fiscal year 1984. President Reagan's conclusion was:

'Taken together, I believe these proposals will put the Nation on a fundamentally different course—a course that will lead to less inflation, more growth, and a brighter future for all our citizens'.

I shall consider how far Thatcherism embodied the same principles as Reaganomics, how far the UK practice corresponded to President Reagan's policy intentions, and how far the outcome in the UK achieved the success promised by the President.

The Origins of Thatcherism

William Niskanen was able to write a valuable book on Reaganomics by reference to one single document which embodied its main ideas.[2] I do not think it would be possible to do the same for Thatcherism. There are a number of reasons for this. The first is that we do not have a Presidential system of government and cannot therefore readily detach the views of the Prime Minister from the views of his or her party. The second is that in Britain the conduct of economic policy is largely the function of a single powerful department, namely the Treasury, and the Prime Minister is not expected to be an independent source of ideas on economic matters. Although it is true (as she sometimes reminds her Cabinet colleagues) that she is First Lord of the Treasury, Mrs Thatcher is not continuously involved in either the formulation or the execution of economic policy. Finally, the pragmatic tradition of British politics militates against the production of written statements which might prove embarrassing later when circumstances change. Thatcherism, like the British system of law, has evolved mainly without codification.

Nevertheless there are two ways in which one is justified in naming the Conservative Government's economic policies after Mrs Thatcher. The first is that many elements of the policies reflect her personal

---

[2] *America's New Beginning: A Program for Economic Recovery*, Washington DC: US Government Printing Office, 1981.

instincts and beliefs. The second is that, but for her determined support, major parts of the programme would have been abandoned when they first encountered difficulties in 1980 and 1981. Mrs Thatcher is certainly the heroine of this story.

Precursors to Thatcherism can be traced to 1970. The Conservative manifesto for the 1970 election, drafted at a meeting at the Selsdon Park Hotel, contained a recognisably liberal declaration:

'... we reject the detailed intervention of socialism, which usurps the function of management, and seeks to dictate prices and earnings in industry. We much prefer a system of general pressures, creating an economic climate which favours and rewards enterprise and efficiency. Our aim is to identify and remove obstacles that prevent effective competition and restrict initiative'.

In the event, the Conservative Government of 1970-74 was the most corporatist of the post-war years. Its economic policies ended in disaster and the Conservative Party lost two elections in succession. Not surprisingly, Mr Heath lost the leadership of the party and his ideas were rejected. During the years of opposition new policies were formulated. One example was *The Right Approach to the Economy*,[3] published in 1977. It called for another 'break for freedom' like the one made by the Conservatives when they regained power in 1951.

'The right approach'

Its major proposals included:

o Strict control by the government of the rate of growth of the money supply.

o Firm management of government expenditure, to reduce the burden on the economy and leave more in people's pockets.

o Lower taxation on earnings, capital and savings, to increase the rewards of skill and enterprise—paving the way to more secure jobs, particularly for the young.

o The removal of unnecessary restrictions on business expansion, to encourage new firms and new work opportunities, rather than excessive preoccupation with existing 'problem areas'.

---

[3] Angus Maude (ed.), *The Right Approach to the Economy: Outline of an Economic Strategy for the Next Conservative Government*, London: Conservative & Unionist Party, 1977.

The Conservative Manifesto of 1979 embodied many of the ideas presented in *The Right Approach to the Economy*. It described Britain as 'a great country which seems to have lost its way'. Among the ways in which Labour Governments had made things worse was the following:

'by enlarging the role of the state and diminishing the role of the individual, they have crippled the enterprise and effort on which a prosperous country with improving social services depends'.

The Manifesto set five tasks, of which the first two were:

'To restore the health of our economic and social life, by controlling inflation and striking a fair balance between the rights and duties of the trade union movement.

'To restore incentives so that hard work pays, success is rewarded and genuine new jobs are created in an expanding economy.'

In the context of a discussion of Reaganomics, the concern with the trade union movement may seem a particularly British obsession, but such concern was understandable in the conditions of 1979.

Inflation was to be cut by monetary means, with publicly stated targets for the growth of the money supply. The control of the money supply was to be accompanied by a gradual reduction in the size of the public sector borrowing requirement (PSBR).

Incentives were to be restored by cuts in income tax.

Within a few weeks of winning the 1979 General Election the Conservatives introduced a Budget in which they fulfilled their promise to cut income tax. At the same time they raised (by nearly 100 per cent) the rate of VAT. That switch from direct to indirect taxation was proposed in *The Right Approach to the Economy*. (Sir Geoffrey Howe, who was one of the authors of that pamphlet, was the first Chancellor of the Exchequer of Mrs Thatcher's Government.) In the conditions of 1979, since it was impossible to cut public spending at short notice, it was essential to raise additional revenue from other sources. The switch from direct to indirect taxation could also be defended in terms of its potential effects on savings.

Approach to public spending

The Government's approach to public spending was set out in a brief White Paper (Cmnd. 7746) published in November 1979. Its opening words were: 'Public expenditure is at the heart of Britain's present economic difficulties'. Support for that bold statement was presented as follows:

> 'Over the years public spending has been increased on assumptions about economic growth which have not been achieved. The inevitable result has been a growing burden of taxes and borrowing.
>
> 'Increases in taxes have made inflationary pressures worse and reduced incentives.
>
> 'High Government borrowing has fuelled inflation, complicated the task of controlling the money supply, raised interest rates and thus denied the wealth-creating sectors some of the external finance they need for expansion.
>
> 'High inflation has increased the risks and uncertainty faced by both employer and employee and gravely damaged investment, production and jobs.
>
> 'If this continued, our economy would be threatened with endemic inflation and economic decline'.[4]

It is interesting that it is the macro-economic rather than the micro-economic effects of public spending which are emphasised here. Public spending is bad because it causes inflation if the economy is not growing rapidly enough. Alternatively, if inflation is to be avoided, taxes have to be raised; but that in turn causes other problems. There is not a strong sense that the size of the public sector represents a mistaken view of the economic role of the state. The same is true of the *Public Expenditure* White Paper of March 1980. It is only slowly that the Conservative Government has moved to the view that there are general questions about the role of public expenditure.

The Nature of Thatcherism

As the Conservative Government's policies have evolved it has been possible to discern a number of themes which can be identified with Thatcherism. I shall discuss two related ones which I believe have provided the strongest contrast with the post-war tradition of policy-making. The first can be called Disengagement and the second Consumerism.

Disengagement refers to the withdrawal of the government from

---

[4] Cmnd. 7746.

areas of economic intervention and responsibility which previous administrations had occupied. The major examples are as follows:

o responsibility for the level of real output and employment;

o direct intervention in the determination of incomes and prices;

o concern with the distribution of income and wealth;

o intervention in the nature and location of economic activity;

o direct involvement in the production of goods and services.

The one responsibility that the Government has retained, and indeed emphasised, throughout its term of office has been the responsibility for controlling inflation. (In his lecture to the Institute of Economic Affairs, *The State of the Market*,[5] Mr Nigel Lawson also claimed that the Government should accept responsibility for the exchange rate, but that is a rather more controversial matter.)

The changed approach to macro-economic policy was, in the early days, the most notable feature of Thatcherism. Both objectives and methods changed. As Mr Lawson explained in the 1984 Mais Lecture,[6] the tools of macro-economic policy were now being directed at controlling inflation whereas the tools of micro-economic policy were now being directed at influencing (but certainly not controlling) the level of output and employment. That was a complete reversal of the previous tradition in which the government used macro-economic policy in an attempt to achieve targets in relation to growth and employment and sought to control inflation by direct means (including prices and incomes policies).

From fiscal to monetary policy

The change in techniques consisted of a switch from reliance on fiscal policy as a means of managing the overall level of demand to the use of monetary policy. The role of fiscal policy is now seen to be concerned with supply-side effects. The overall fiscal balance (as measured by the PSBR) is judged in relation to long-term objectives, for example, in relation to the size of the national debt. The conduct of monetary policy has been modified somewhat since 1979, partly in response to the structural changes which influenced the demand for broad money (M3) which was originally chosen as the indicator of monetary

---

[5] Occasional Paper 80, London: Institute of Economic Affairs, 1988.

[6] *The British Economic Experiment*, London: HM Treasury, 1984.

conditions. In recent years the main intermediate target has become the growth of nominal demand as measured by 'Money GDP', or GDP in current prices.

The last three elements of disengagement reflect the micro-economic aspects of Thatcherism. Since 1979 there has been a significant widening in the distribution of income. A widening of the distribution of pre-tax pay has been reinforced by cuts in all tax rates, particularly at the highest levels. The Conservatives have regarded the restoration of incentives as more important than the achievement of equality. Regional policy has not been abandoned, but it has been greatly changed and is no longer concerned with the maintenance of a particular pattern of production and employment (most notably in manufacturing). Privatisation which at one stage seemed to be the archetypical feature of Thatcherism, challenges, in the most obvious way, the role of the state as a direct producer of goods and services.

Thus the process of disengagement has greatly reduced the economic role of the state and the process is not yet at an end.

Thatcherism and Consumerism

I have suggested that consumerism is the second outstanding feature of Thatcherism. It could be argued that it is the *essential* feature of Thatcherism and that disengagement follows logically from it. By consumerism I mean that policies are designed to recognise the preferences of consumers rather than producers. At the best of times, governments and political parties will be far more likely to respond to producer interests than to consumer interests. The problem is even more serious when we have interventionist governments since it will be the producers who tell the government how to intervene. This is all well recognised now, largely thanks to the work of Professor Buchanan and his colleagues.

It is to the everlasting credit of Mrs Thatcher and the Conservative Government that they have reversed the post-war tradition. It was a tradition which reached its low point during the Conservative administration of 1970-74 when there was an attempt at tripartite government with the CBI, the TUC and the civil servants deciding how large GDP should be and how it should be shared out. It was ironic that at the time of the miners' strike Mr Heath called a general election to decide who ran the country, the unions or the government. To paraphrase Bernard Shaw, we already knew the answer to that, the only question was the price. (It may be noted in passing that Mrs Thatcher's attention to consumer rather than producer preferences extends far beyond matters to do with economic policy. She has been far from popular, for instance, in those monuments to producer interests, the universities and the BBC.)

Casualties of Unemployment

Of course, most people are both producers and consumers and policies that favour consumers will produce casualties. The outstanding example of the conflict relates to unemployment. I have suggested that one aspect of disengagement has been the withdrawal from responsibility for the level of employment. It is true that micro-economic policies have been directed towards improving the working of the labour market but the short-term effect of such policies can be to raise unemployment. The withdrawal of the commitment to full employment was crucial both in terms of the counter-inflationary policy and in terms of the attempt to improve the supply-side performance of the economy. A government committed to full employment cannot control inflation since it must adjust policies to accommodate whatever wages the trade unions are able to set. At the same time managers will respond to the full-employment policy and will, reasonably enough, assume that they can best contribute to economic welfare by employing people.

The break-through which produced the supply-side revolution was achieved in 1980 when employers, particularly in manufacturing, realised that firms could survive only if employment levels were drastically cut. The Government, remarkably, did not change its policies as unemployment rose at an unprecedented rate and, in fact, pursued its counter-inflation policy vigorously with the tough Budget of 1981. The benefit to consumers has been clear; but we must not forget the producers who have lost.

I believe it is an open question how far de-regulation and trade union reform led to this result. I share Patrick Minford's view that the reforms have made it far more difficult for the unions to resist labour-shedding. There is a long list of failed attempts (from the steel workers, through the coal miners and the printers to the ferry-workers) to maintain employment at uneconomic levels.

Thatcherism in Practice

I have suggested that Thatcherism has much in common with Reaganomics. In the UK, as in the USA, the objectives of economic

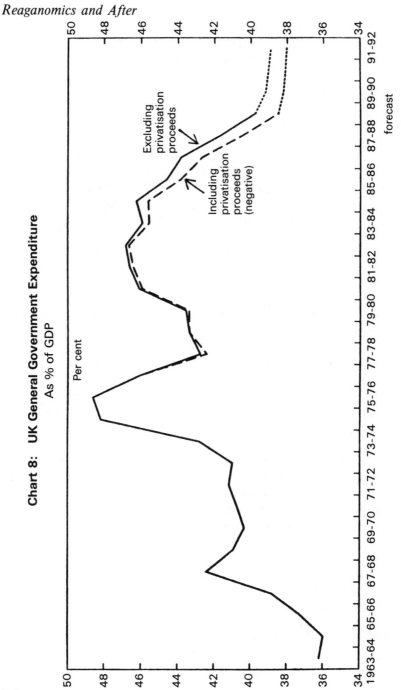

Chart 8: UK General Government Expenditure
As % of GDP

Per cent

Excluding privatisation proceeds

Including privatisation proceeds (negative)

forecast

Chart 9: Public Sector Borrowing and Financial Deficit
As % Money GDP

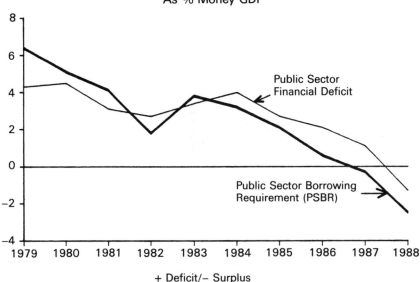

+ Deficit/– Surplus

policy have been to reduce the economic role of the state, to restore incentives and to cut inflation. It may be helpful to judge the achievements of the Conservative Government by reference to the objectives set out in President Reagan's Programme for Economic Recovery.

Like President Reagan, the Conservative Government started with the ambition of curbing the growth of public spending. Its original ambition, as set out in the 1980 *Public Expenditure* White Paper, was to reduce total spending absolutely in real terms. Subsequently its ambitions have been rather more modest. Chart 8 (taken from the Autumn statement) shows that, after a period in which general government expenditure rose in relation to GDP, its share was held and then sharply reduced. Expenditure on goods and services has fallen steadily as a share of GDP. The change in the financial position of the public sector has been even more dramatic. The PSBR and the Budget deficit have both moved into surplus (Chart 9).

Cutting public spending is only one aspect of reducing the economic role of the government; but it is the most readily measured. It is difficult to know how to quantify de-regulation and even more difficult to know whether President Reagan was more successful than Mrs

Chart 10: Growth in Monetary Aggregates
Annual % Changes

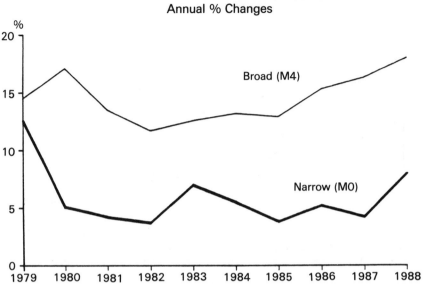

Thatcher. The same goes for changes in taxation. One can perhaps argue that President Reagan's proposals have been more radical while the Conservatives have achieved the largest reduction in the top marginal rates.

Monetary Growth

The chosen method of controlling inflation has been monetary policy. Charts 10 to 12 show what has happened to monetary growth and interest rates. The monetary indicator chosen originally (M3) proved to be particularly subject to institutional change. Chart 10 shows a rather more representative broad money indicator (M4) and the chosen indicator of narrow money (MO). Charts 11 and 12 show that, despite the considerable tightening of fiscal policy, real interest rates have remained high throughout most of the period.

President Reagan promised less inflation, more growth and a brighter future for all citizens. Charts 13 and 14 provide some evidence of Mrs Thatcher's achievements in relation to the first two objectives. There is no doubt of the success in cutting inflation. On growth, experience since 1982 has far exceeded the average growth of the 1970s, but one must recognise the lost output of 1980 and 1981. One

[continued on page 109]

Chart 11:   UK Nominal Interest Rates
3-Month Interbank

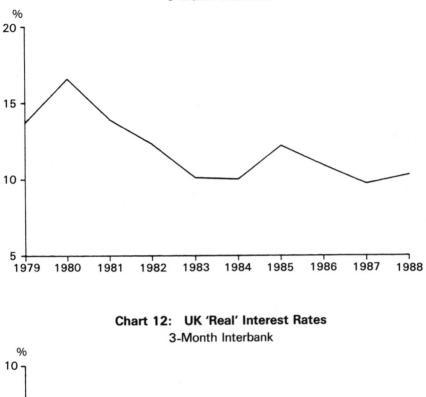

Chart 12:   UK 'Real' Interest Rates
3-Month Interbank

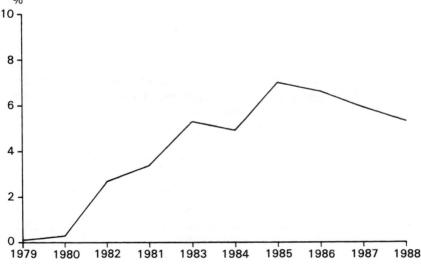

Chart 13: UK Consumer Price Inflation
1970-79 v 1980-88

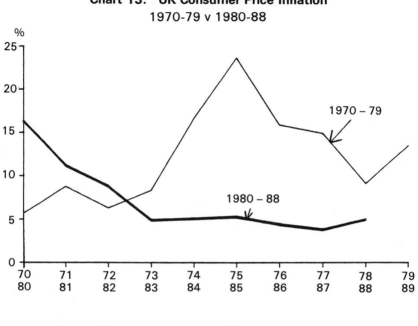

1970 – 79

1980 – 88

| 70 | 71 | 72 | 73 | 74 | 75 | 76 | 77 | 78 | 79 |
| 80 | 81 | 82 | 83 | 84 | 85 | 86 | 87 | 88 | 89 |

Chart 14: UK Non-Oil GDP
1970-79 v 1980-88

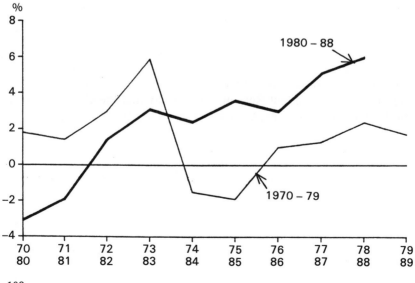

1980 – 88

1970 – 79

| 70 | 71 | 72 | 73 | 74 | 75 | 76 | 77 | 78 | 79 |
| 80 | 81 | 82 | 83 | 84 | 85 | 86 | 87 | 88 | 89 |

Chart 15: UK Adult Unemployment
1970-79 v 1980-88

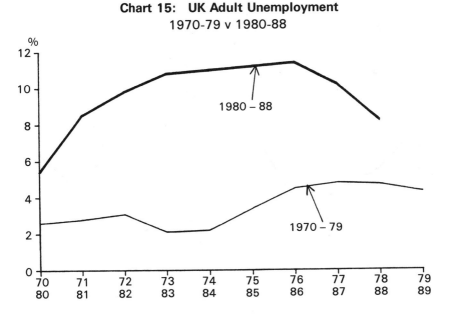

could hardly hope to find a single chart which measured the brightness of the citizens' future. Chart 15 does provide a reminder that not all the members of the community have gained from these policies. That provides the sharpest contrast with the United States where near-full employment was rapidly restored. It suggests that we have not solved all our supply-side problems.

In summary, I suggest that the UK has generally experienced a successful experiment in Reaganomics. Perhaps, since the principles and intentions are so similar and since Mrs Thatcher came to power 20 months before President Reagan, one can say that the USA has had a moderately successful experiment in Thatcherism.

THE AUTHORS

Sir Alan Peacock is Executive Director of the David Hume Institute, Edinburgh, and Research Professor of Public Finance at the Esmee Fairbairn Research Centre, Heriot-Watt University, Edinburgh. He was Chairman of the Committee on the Financing of the BBC (which produced the 'Peacock Report', 1986), and formerly Principal and Professor of Economics, University College at Buckingham, 1978-83; Professor of Economics and Head of Department of Economics, University of York, 1962-77; Chief Economic Adviser, Departments of Industry, Trade and Prices and Consumer Protection, 1973-76. Formerly a member of the IEA Advisory Council, now a Trustee of the IEA. Author of numerous books, including *Economic Analysis of Government* (1979); *Economy of Taxation* (1981); *The Regulation Game* (1984); *Public Expenditure and Government Growth* (1985); (with Jack Wiseman) *The Growth of Public Expenditure in the UK* (1961); *Income Redistribution and Social Policy* (1954); (with G. K. Shaw) *Fiscal Policy and the Employment Problem* (1971); co-author (with C. K. Rowley) of *Welfare Economics: A Liberal Restatement* (1975). For the IEA he has written: (with Jack Wiseman) *Education for Democrats* (Hobart Paper 25, 1964); (with A. J. Culyer) *Economic Aspects of Student Unrest* (Occasional Paper 26, 1969); *The Credibility of Liberal Economics* (Seventh Wincott Memorial Lecture, Occasional Paper 50, 1977); 'Trade Unions and Economic Policy', in *Trade Unions: Public Goods or Public 'Bads'?* (Readings 17, 1978).

James M. Buchanan is a Nobel Laureate and the Harris University Professor and Advisory General Director, Center for Study of Public Choice, George Mason University. He was formerly University Distinguished Professor of Economics and General Director of the Center for Study of Public Choice at the Virginia Polytechnic Institute, Blacksburg, Virginia; Professor of Economics at Florida State University, 1951-56; University of Virginia (and Director of the Thomas Jefferson Center for Political Economy), 1956-68; University of California at Los Angeles, 1968-69. He is the author of numerous

111

works on aspects of the economics of politics and public choice, including (with Gordon Tullock) *The Calculus of Consent* (1962); *Public Finance in Democratic Process* (1967); *Demand and Supply of Public Goods* (1968); *The Limits of Liberty: Between Anarchy and Leviathan* (1975); and (with Richard E. Wagner) *Democracy in Deficit: The Political Legacy of Lord Keynes* (1977). Professor Buchanan is a member of the IEA's Advisory Council. The IEA has published his *The Inconsistencies of the National Health Service* (Occasional Paper 7, 1965); (with Richard E. Wagner and John Burton) *The Consequences of Mr Keynes* (Hobart Paper 78, 1978); 'From Private Preference to Public Philosophy: The Development of Public Choice', in *The Economics of Politics* (Readings 18, 1978); and 'Our Times: Past, Present, and Future' in *The Unfinished Agenda* (1986).

William A. Niskanen, Jr. is Chairman of the Cato Institute, Washington DC, and formerly Professor of Economics, Graduate School of Public Policy, University of California, Berkeley, 1972-75. Previously Rand Corporation, 1957-61; Office of the Secretary of Defense, 1962-64; Institute for Defense Analyses, 1965-70. Assistant Director for Evaluation in the Federal Office of Management and Budget, Washington, 1970-72; Director of Economics, Ford Motor, 1975-80; Professor, Graduate School of Management, UCLA, 1980-81. From 1981 to 1985 he served as a member of President Reagan's Council of Economic Advisers and as acting Chairman. Author of *Reaganomics: An Insider's Account of the Policies and the People* (1988); *Bureaucracy and Representative Government* (1972). For the IEA he has written *Bureaucracy: Servant or Master?* (Hobart Paperback 5, 1973); and 'Competition Among Government Bureaus', in *The Economics of Politics* (Readings 18, 1978).

Paul Craig Roberts is William E. Simon Professor of Political Economy at the Center for Strategic & International Studies (CSIS) in Washington DC, and Senior Research Fellow in the Hoover Institution, Stanford University. Dr Roberts was educated at the Georgia Institute of Technology, the University of Virginia, the University of California at Berkeley, and Oxford University, where he was a member of Merton College. During 1981-82 he served as Assistant Secretary of the Treasury for Economic Policy. During 1975-78 he served on the Congressional staff where he drafted the Kemp-Roth Bill and played a leading role in developing bipartisan support for a supply-side economic policy. He is the author of *The Supply-Side Revolution* (1984), *Alienation and the Soviet Economy* (1971), and *Marx's Theory of Exchange, Alienation, and Crisis* (1973), as well as numerous articles in the learned journals, including the *Journal of Political Economy*, *Journal of Law and Economics*, *Journal of Monetary Economics*, *Public Choice*, and *Oxford Economic Papers*.

A. P. L. (Patrick) Minford has been Edward Gonner Professor of Applied Economics, University of Liverpool, since 1976. Formerly Visiting Hallsworth Research Fellow, University of Manchester, 1974-75. Sometime Consultant to the Ministry of Overseas Development, Ministry of Finance (Malawi), Courtaulds, Treasury, British Embassy (Washington). Editor of *National Institute Economic Review*, 1975-76. He is the author of *Substitution Effects, Speculation and Exchange Rate Stability* (1978), and of essays published in *Inflation in Open Economies* (1976); *The Effects of Exchange Adjustments* (1977); *On How to Cope with Britain's Trade Position* (1977); *Contemporary Economic Analysis* (1978); co-author of *Unemployment: Cause and Cure* (1983, 2nd edn. 1985). He is a member of the IEA's Advisory Council and has contributed papers to *The Taming of Government* (IEA Readings 21, 1979); *Is Monetarism Enough?* (IEA Readings 24, 1980); *Could Do Better* (Occasional Paper 62, 1982); and *The Unfinished Agenda* (1986). He was joint author (with Michael Peel and Paul Ashton) of *The Housing Morass* (Hobart Paperback 25, IEA, 1987) and edited and introduced *Monetarism and Macro-economics* (IEA Readings 26, 1987).

Dr Irwin M. Stelzer is Director of Harvard University's Energy and Environmental Policy Center; US economic correspondent for the *Sunday Times*; and Associate Member of Nuffield College, Oxford. He founded National Economic Research Associates, Inc. (NERA) in 1961 and served as its President until a few years after its sale in 1983 to Marsh & McLennan. He was a Managing Director of Rothschild Inc., investment bankers, and is now a Director of Putnam, Hayes & Bartlett, Inc. Dr Stelzer has served on numerous government committees investigating the regulated industries and competition policy and as a consultant to most of America's regulated companies. He has been named to the Advisory Panel of the President's National Commission for the Review of Antitrust Laws and Procedures. He has published work on competition in regulated industries, the organisation of cable broadcasting and antitrust economics. He has served as

Economic Editor of the *Antitrust Bulletin*, is a member of the Editorial Board of *Telematics*, and is the author of *Selected Antitrust Cases: Landmark Decisions* (7th edition, 1986).

Alan Budd is Chief Economic Adviser to Barclays Bank. He was previously Professor of Economics at the London Business School (1981-88) and is now Visiting Professor there. He was Senior Economic Adviser to the Treasury (1970-74), and taught at the University of Southampton (1966-69). He has been a Visiting Professor at Carnegie-Mellon University (1969-70) and at the University of New South Wales (1983). He is a member of the IEA's Advisory Council and has contributed to a number of its collections: *The Taming of Government* (Readings 21, 1979); *Keynes's General Theory: Fifty Years On* (Hobart Paperback 24, 1986); *Monetarism and Macro-economics* (Readings 26, 1987); he also contributed a Commentary to *The State of the Market* (Occasional Paper 80, 1988).

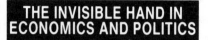